OTHER BOOKS
BY THE ROBERTSON FAMILY

The Duck Commander Family

Happy, Happy, Happy

Si-cology 1

The Duck Commander Devotional
(also available in pink camo and leather-touch)

Miss Kay's Duck Commander Kitchen

Everything's Better with a Beard

The Women of DUCK COMMANDER

---

*Surprising Insights from the
Women Behind the Beards About What
Makes This Family Work*

**Kay Robertson, Korie Robertson,
Missy Robertson, Jessica Robertson,
and Lisa Robertson**

with **Beth Clark**

HOWARD BOOKS
A DIVISION OF SIMON & SCHUSTER, INC.

New York   Nashville   London   Toronto   Sydney   New Delhi

Howard Books
A Division of Simon & Schuster, Inc.
1230 Avenue of the Americas
New York, NY 10020

First Howard Books hardcover edition April 2014

HOWARD and colophon are trademarks of Simon & Schuster, Inc.

For information about special discounts for bulk purchases, please contact Simon & Schuster Special Sales at 1-866-506-1949 or business@simonandschuster.com.

The Simon & Schuster Speakers Bureau can bring authors to your live event. For more information or to book an event, contact the Simon & Schuster Speakers Bureau at 1-866-248-3049 or visit our website at www.simonspeakers.com.

Interior design by Jaime Putorti
Jacket design by Bruce Gore
Jacket photographs © Steven Palowsky

Manufactured in the United States of America

10 9 8 7 6 5 4 3 2 1

Library of Congress Cataloging-in-Publication Data
Robertson, Kay.
  The women of Duck Commander : surprising insights from the women behind the beards about what makes this family work / Kay Robertson, Korie Robertson, Missy Robertson, Jessica Robertson, and Lisa Robertson ; with Beth Clark. — First Howard Books hardcover edition.
      pages cm
1. Robertson, Kay. 2. Robertson, Kay—Family. 3. Robertson, Korie. 4. Robertson, Korie—Family. 5. Robertson, Missy. 6. Robertson, Missy—Family. 7. Robertson, Jessica. 8. Robertson, Jessica—Family. 9. Robertson, Lisa. 10. Robertson, Lisa—Family. 11. Television personalities—United States—Biography. 12. Duck dynasty (Television program) I. Robertson, Korie. II. Robertson, Missy. III. Robertson, Jessica. IV. Robertson, Lisa. V. Clark, Beth. VI. Title.
  PN1992.4.R534A3 2014
  791.4502'809252—dc23
  [B]
                                        2013039886
ISBN 978-1-4767-6330-9
ISBN 978-1-4767-6357-6 (ebook)

Dedication

We would like to dedicate this book to the main men in our lives: Phil, Alan, Jase, Willie, and Jep. You love us, support us, and keep us laughing. We love you, respect you, and feel blessed to be your soul mates. Life with you is never boring.

We also give thanks and honor to our Lord Jesus Christ for giving us this opportunity to share our faith with the world. Without His sacrifice on the cross we would not have the hope of eternal life.

The Gospel

Jesus came ↓   Jesus died ✝   Jesus was buried ⌒   Jesus went to heaven ↗   Jesus is coming back to get us! ↓

The simple story of Jesus.
Love, Miss Kay

Television is what we do; faith is who we are.

—*The Robertson wives*

CONTENTS

Part One

HOW I BECAME A ROBERTSON

Part Two
NO ORDINARY IN-LAWS

Part Three
HAPPILY EVER AFTER CAN TAKE A WHILE

Part Four
TALKIN' ABOUT MY GENERATIONS

CONTENTS

Part Five

SOMETIMES MIRACLES HIDE

Part Six

LIFE IN THE LIMELIGHT

Part Seven

INQUIRING MINDS WANT TO KNOW

FOREWORD

The distinct sound of a duck call pierced the quiet of the commuter jet cabin just before we landed in Monroe, Louisiana. *At least I know I'm in the right place*, I thought as I joined my fellow passengers in applause. I don't know how many people's travels that day would have anything to do with *Duck Dynasty* or the Robertson family, but everyone on the flight seemed excited to have finally arrived in the lush green bayou country the Robertsons call home.

As I made my way toward West Monroe to meet the Robertson women for the first time, I had some of the same questions much of America has about them: Are they really who they seem to be—down-to-earth, sincere, commonsense, loving wives and mothers? Do the women really get along and support each other? Do they really love their family as much as the show portrays? Are their children truly as respectful as they come across? And is their sense of humor what the show would have an audience think? In a word, yes. Definitely yes.

Within a few minutes of sitting down for a meal with these women, I began to see that they are the real deal—warm, friendly, gracious, humble, fun, passionate about God, devoted to family, and altogether genuine. There's no pretense in the Robertson wives. Each one is strong, smart, talented, and enormously capable in her own right, and each keeps the family fame in perspective. While they appreciate the chance to be on a television show that breaks ratings records and makes history, they're not impressed with themselves; they are focused on the things that really matter. They are committed to timeless values, and they are wholly true to a strong set of unshakable convictions, convictions based on the ancient, proven truth of Scripture. They have learned the hard way that a life of faith is not always easy, but it *is* always good.

In this book, the Robertson wives are happy to share the stories, insights, and experiences that have made them who they are. With transparency, humility, and forthrightness, they write about the things that have shaped their lives not as television stars, but as human beings—as women who know the same longings and cares, joys and sorrows, victories and struggles as women everywhere. If you have ever wondered why they are the way they are, you'll find answers in these pages. If you want to move toward a greater commitment to faith, family, and the things that make life truly rich, you will find direction here.

This behind-the-scenes look into the Robertson women's world is not just made of words; it's made of influence. Its stories and lessons have the power to shape your life in the most positive ways and the potential to lead you and others into the kind of good life and values-based living that is the foundation of the Robertsons' success.

The Robertson wives are not clamoring for the spotlight but cooperating with the spotlight, because they understand that for a moment in television history they are part of something that calls millions of people back to the basic goodness of life—and they share that goodness with humor and self-effacing honesty. They don't pay too much attention to what the world says is important. Their must-haves are not designer clothes or luxury cars. Their must-haves are love, loyalty, kindness, forgiveness, generosity, respect, honest hard work, care for others, and a host of other virtues. The unprecedented popularity of *Duck Dynasty* makes me wonder if, at the end of the day, these simple qualities are what the heart of America really longs for.

The whole *Duck Dynasty* phenomenon is a bit of a revolution. It's certainly turned the world of entertainment on its ear and challenged what many media insiders think America wants to watch. They're finding out that clean humor, marital fidelity, and prayer before a meal can trump sex, violence, and bad language. The funny thing is, the revolution of *Duck Dynasty* is not leading us into anything new; it's simply taking us back to some things our culture is in danger of losing—love, laughter, family, and faith. In the Robertson women these things run deeper than any once-a-week television show could ever convey; they are the very fabric of their lives.

Beth Clark
Nashville, Tennessee

Introducing

THE DUCK COMMANDER WOMEN

Kay Robertson
(OTHERWISE KNOWN AS "MISS KAY")

BORN AND RAISED IN: Born in Vivian, Louisiana; raised in Ida, Louisiana

HUSBAND'S NAME: Phil Alexander Robertson

CHILDREN'S NAMES AND BIRTH YEARS:
Alan (born 1965)
Jason (we call him Jase; born 1969)
Willie (born 1972)
Jeptha (we call him Jep; born 1978)

HUSBAND'S BEST QUALITY: His passionate faith and charismatic personality

FAVORITE DUCK DISH: Duck wraps, though I like pretty much everything if it's made of duck

LEAST-FAVORITE FOOD: I haven't yet met a food I didn't like

TALENT NOT VERY MANY PEOPLE KNOW ABOUT: I can draw and paint

FAVORITE COLOR: Blue

FAVORITE VACATION DESTINATION: Gulf Shores, Alabama

FAVORITE SCRIPTURE: Philippians 4:13, NKJV: "I can do all things through Christ who strengthens me."

FAVORITE SONG: "Amazing Grace," the old version and the new one

THE BEST THING ABOUT BEING A ROBERTSON IS: We have a heritage of faith

THREE THINGS I'M THANKFUL FOR:

1. Family: my husband, children, grandchildren, and great-grandchildren
2. My grandmother, who shared her faith with me, and my sister, Ann, who is one of my best friends
3. Living in America

MORNING PERSON OR NIGHT PERSON? Night person

ONE THING THAT REALLY GETS ON MY NERVES: Disrespectful children and adults

ONE THING ON MY BUCKET LIST: To have a great seat at a New Orleans Saints football game and to visit with the team

ONE PERSON I REALLY ADMIRE AND WHY: My son Alan. He did not get to have a childhood or do many of the things little boys often get to enjoy doing. He never resented the problems and struggles he had to deal with for ten years during a difficult time in our family's life.

HOW I FEEL ABOUT HOUSEWORK: I'm not fond of it. I feel blessed to be able to have a housekeeper. Here's a quick story to make my point. A little girl and her mother came to see me one day. When the girl looked around my house, she said, "Miss Kay, somebody done come here and messed up your how-se!" Her mother was so embarrassed. I wasn't. I just smiled and said, "Look, we live in this house. We do the best we can, and we have a housekeeper." I guess the house-keeper had not been there that day. I absolutely loved that child's honesty.

TOTAL NUMBER OF DAYS SPENT IN A DUCK BLIND: One

BEST ADVICE ANYONE EVER GAVE ME: My grandmother told me, "You're going to have to fight for your marriage."

WORST ADVICE ANYONE EVER GAVE ME: "Leave Phil" (when times were tough)

MY GRANDMOTHER ALWAYS SAID: "Pretty is as pretty does."

I WOULD NEVER LEAVE THE HOUSE WITHOUT: My sense of humor and my American Express card

MY FAVORITE THING TO DO DURING DUCK SEASON IS: Sleep in and go shopping

IF I COULD DO ONE THING TO CHANGE THE WORLD TODAY, I WOULD: Love all the people who have no one to love them and feed as many as I could

WHEN I WAS LITTLE, I WANTED TO GROW UP AND BE: A somewhat modern pioneer woman who became a great wife and mother, had a lot of animals to love, and was the best cook around. I always wanted to have a smile on my face and to be pleasant at all times.

Lisa Robertson

BORN AND RAISED IN: West Monroe, Louisiana

HUSBAND'S NAME: Marshal Alan Robertson

CHILDREN'S NAMES AND BIRTH YEARS:
Anna (born 1986)
Alex (born 1987)

GRANDCHILDREN: Carley Elizabeth Stone (born 2005), Bailey Kay Stone (born 2007), Corban Marshal Mancuso, to be named after Alan (due March 2014), and another on the way

HUSBAND'S BEST QUALITY: His forgiving heart

FAVORITE DUCK DISH: Duck and dressing

LEAST-FAVORITE FOOD: Crawfish. It's a long story.

TALENT NOT VERY MANY PEOPLE KNOW ABOUT: My Mexican corn bread is better than Miss Kay's (and even Miss Kay agrees)!

FAVORITE COLOR: Purple

FAVORITE VACATION DESTINATION: Anywhere on the beach

FAVORITE SCRIPTURE: Proverbs 24:26, NIV 2011: "An honest answer is like a kiss on the lips."

FAVORITE SONG: "Someone Like You" by Adele

THE BEST THING ABOUT BEING A ROBERTSON IS: Being married to Alan

THREE THINGS I'M THANKFUL FOR:

1. Salvation
2. Love
3. Family

MORNING PERSON OR NIGHT PERSON? I'm a midday person, or a "pretty much anytime" person

ONE THING THAT REALLY GETS ON MY NERVES: People who make fun of those who are disabled or mentally challenged

ONE THING ON MY BUCKET LIST: To live to see my great-great-grandchildren

ONE PERSON I REALLY ADMIRE AND WHY: Lynda Hammitt, a friend and coworker at Duck Commander. She has been to hell and back, and lived to witness about it. Her positive attitude is amazing!

HOW I FEEL ABOUT HOUSEWORK: I don't mind it. I love a clean house.

TOTAL NUMBER OF DAYS SPENT IN A DUCK BLIND: One

BEST ADVICE ANYONE EVER GAVE ME: "Forgive and move on."

WORST ADVICE ANYONE EVER GAVE ME: "Use cloth diapers."

MY GRANDMOTHER ALWAYS SAID: "Eat what's on your plate. There are starving kids who wish they could have what you leave."

I WOULD NEVER LEAVE THE HOUSE WITHOUT: Lipstick

MY FAVORITE THING TO DO DURING DUCK SEASON IS: Sleep in

IF I COULD DO ONE THING TO CHANGE THE WORLD TODAY, I WOULD: Tell everyone about Jesus and His love, grace, and salvation

WHEN I WAS LITTLE, I WANTED TO GROW UP AND BE: A nurse. I wanted to be a nurse until I became a mom—and then I knew I couldn't handle it.

Melissa "Missy" Louise West Robertson

BORN AND RAISED IN: Lubbock, Texas, but moved to West Monroe, Louisiana, when I was six months old

HUSBAND'S NAME: Jason Silas "Jase" Robertson

CHILDREN'S NAMES AND BIRTH YEARS:
Reed Silas (born 1995)
Cole Foster (born 1997)
Mia Elaine (born 2003)

HUSBAND'S BEST QUALITY: Forgiveness

FAVORITE DUCK DISH: Duck wraps

LEAST-FAVORITE FOOD: Bologna sandwiches. I ate them every day for my school lunch when I was a kid. I can hardly even stomach the smell of them today.

TALENT NOT VERY MANY PEOPLE KNOW ABOUT: Not many people know I sing, have been trained to sing, and have sung my entire life.

FAVORITE COLOR: Green

FAVORITE VACATION DESTINATION: So far? Hawaii, but I plan on exploring this more in the future.

FAVORITE SCRIPTURE: Philippians 2:14: "Do everything without complaining or arguing." I don't always live by it, but I try. I want to be a shining star for Him!

FAVORITE SONG: I love music. I always have. I love eighties pop. I love today's country. I love Christian music. I love big orchestral, classical pieces. I even like some opera. My life has always been full of music.

THE BEST THING ABOUT BEING A ROBERTSON IS: The many people who love and accept me for who I am, faults and all

THREE THINGS I'M THANKFUL FOR:

1. Jesus' sacrifice for me and His consistent love and forgiveness
2. My husband's dedication to me and our family
3. The blessing of family

MORNING PERSON OR NIGHT PERSON? Neither. I require a lot of sleep.

ONE THING THAT REALLY GETS ON MY NERVES: Mumblers. It doesn't matter what people say if no one can understand them!

ONE THING ON MY BUCKET LIST: I really want to visit the Holy Land and see where Jesus walked on the earth

ONE PERSON I REALLY ADMIRE AND WHY: I greatly admire my sister-in-law Lisa. She lived a life of bad choices for a long time, but when she decided to change her life, she truly repented. She is a godly, caring, loving woman, and I am proud to call her my sister.

HOW I FEEL ABOUT HOUSEWORK: I love a clean house! I just hate to clean it. In the past, the first thing I'd splurge on when Jase and I had a little extra money was hiring a housecleaner. I now have it worked into the budget.

TOTAL NUMBER OF DAYS SPENT IN A DUCK BLIND: In twenty-five years with Jase? A grand total of three days. The first time was when Jase and I dated, just to see what he was so obsessed with. The second time was for our first television show on Outdoor Channel. I killed two ducks on that hunt and winged another one. The third time I'll write about later in the book.

BEST ADVICE ANYONE EVER GAVE ME: "The best thing you can do for your kids is to love their daddy."

WORST ADVICE ANYONE EVER GAVE ME: "Go ahead, take a bite. It tastes just like chicken."

MY MOTHER ALWAYS SAID: "If your friends jumped off the Empire State Building, would you?"

I WOULD NEVER LEAVE THE HOUSE WITHOUT: My cell phone

MY FAVORITE THING TO DO DURING DUCK SEASON IS: Eat duck wraps!

WHEN I WAS LITTLE, I WANTED TO GROW UP AND BE: A successful, single woman living in New York City. Then I met Jase.

Korie Robertson

BORN AND RAISED IN: West Monroe, Louisiana

HUSBAND'S NAME: Willie Jess Robertson

CHILDREN'S NAMES AND BIRTH YEARS:

John Luke (born 1995)

Sadie (born 1997)

Will (born 2001)

Bella (born 2002)

Rebecca (born 1988; came to live with us in 2005)

HUSBAND'S BEST QUALITY: Besides always being able to make me laugh, Willie is a great leader for our family and to others. Even as a kid, he always loved to take the underdogs and lead them to victory. And most important is his spiritual leadership in our home. He loves God with all his heart, and it shows in how he lives. Plus he's a great cook! Okay, maybe those are his three best qualities.

FAVORITE DUCK DISH: Duck wraps: duck, jalapeño pepper, and cream cheese wrapped in bacon

LEAST-FAVORITE FOOD: Coconut. I don't like the texture.

TALENT NOT VERY MANY PEOPLE KNOW ABOUT: I can do a backflip on the trampoline and off the diving board.

FAVORITE COLOR: Green

FAVORITE VACATION DESTINATION: Snow skiing, anywhere

FAVORITE SCRIPTURE: Micah 6:8: "He has showed you, O man, what is good. And what does the Lord require of you? To act justly and to love mercy and to walk humbly with your God."

FAVORITE SONG: "Boondocks" by Little Big Town. Sounds a lot like the Robertsons!

THE BEST THING ABOUT BEING A ROBERTSON IS: It's never boring! We laugh a lot. But most important, everyone, and I mean everyone, puts God first—and when you do that it makes your relationships so much better.

THREE THINGS I'M THANKFUL FOR:
1. My family
2. My home
3. Getting to travel

MORNING PERSON OR NIGHT PERSON? Definitely night

ONE THING THAT REALLY GETS ON MY NERVES: Mosquitoes

ONE THING ON MY BUCKET LIST: A visit to Africa

ONE PERSON I REALLY ADMIRE AND WHY: My mom. She is hands-down the most unselfish person I know. She is an awesome example of a godly wife, mom, and friend. She's strong but kind, and she's busy but always has enough time for you. She puts her family first but has big goals and dreams of her own. She has never let me down. Plus, I wish I had her energy. She never stops!

HOW I FEEL ABOUT HOUSEWORK: I'm a disaster at housework. I like to organize, clean out closets, etc., but nothing ever stays that way. It will look great for about two days and then it's right back where we started. We are not good at cleaning up as we go along in our house. I like to enjoy life, then when it gets to a certain level, we have what I call "Family Cleanup Time." I feel like if I'm cleaning, someone else should be too! Plus, it gets done a lot faster if everyone pitches in.

TOTAL NUMBER OF DAYS SPENT IN A DUCK BLIND: One

BEST ADVICE ANYONE EVER GAVE ME: I heard or read somewhere: "A woman can do everything she wants in life, just not all at once." I was a stay-at-home mom when our kids were little and I loved that; wouldn't change it for the world. Now I'm a working mom and I love that too. It's all about balance and patience. You've got a lifetime to reach your goals; don't rush it and put pressure on yourself. You'll just make yourself and everyone around you stressed.

WORST ADVICE ANYONE EVER GAVE ME: To get that short haircut in the eighties. I have a big head and skinny legs. I looked like a Q-tip.

MY MOTHER ALWAYS SAID: "If you can't say something nice, don't say anything at all." This was usually said in reference to how I talked to my siblings or how they talked to me, but the Bible says one should be quick to listen, slow to speak, and slow to become angry, so I think she had something there.

I WOULD NEVER LEAVE THE HOUSE WITHOUT: Lip gloss. I feel naked without something on my lips.

MY FAVORITE THING TO DO DURING DUCK SEASON IS: Go back to sleep after Willie crawls out of bed at four A.M. on those cold, rainy mornings. I've also been known to take a few shopping trips to New York City with the girls during this time!

IF I COULD DO ONE THING TO CHANGE THE WORLD TODAY, I WOULD: Give all the orphans homes with a loving family.

WHEN I WAS LITTLE, I WANTED TO GROW UP AND BE: A stockbroker (not sure why), an art teacher, and a model—but mostly a mom.

Jessica Robertson

BORN AND RAISED IN: Born in Bossier, Louisiana; raised in West Monroe, Louisiana

HUSBAND: Jules Jeptha (Jep) Robertson

CHILDREN'S NAMES AND BIRTH YEARS:
Lillian (Lily) Mae (born 2002)
Merritt Decatur (born 2004)
Priscilla June (born 2006)
River Alexander (born 2008)

HUSBAND'S BEST QUALITY: Jep has such a big heart, a heart after God

FAVORITE DUCK DISH: Duck wraps

LEAST-FAVORITE FOOD: Barbecue

TALENT NOT MANY PEOPLE KNOW ABOUT: I can sew really well

FAVORITE COLOR: Red

FAVORITE VACATION ACTIVITY: Snow skiing

FAVORITE SCRIPTURE: 3 John 4: "I have no greater joy than to hear that my children are walking in the truth."

FAVORITE SONG: "(Sitting On) The Dock of the Bay" by Otis Redding

THE BEST THING ABOUT BEING A ROBERTSON IS: The abundant love and all the encouragement we share

THREE THINGS I'M THANKFUL FOR:
1. The death, burial, and resurrection of Jesus Christ
2. My husband and my children
3. Family, friends, and other church family

MORNING PERSON OR NIGHT PERSON: Although I grew up a morning person (I was usually in bed by nine P.M.), Jep turned me into a night person. My junior and senior years, I took seven A.M. classes (that's how much of a morning person I was). Now I can't seem to get up before seven.

ONE THING THAT REALLY GETS ON MY NERVES: Smacking!!

ONE THING ON MY BUCKET LIST: A vacation in Italy

ONE PERSON I REALLY ADMIRE AND WHY: My mamaw Nellie Fincher. I have learned so much from her about commitment, love, Jesus, selflessness, and true joy. She loves Jesus Christ more than anything or anyone else. She is the most influential woman in my life.

HOW I FEEL ABOUT HOUSEWORK: I really don't like housework; I hate it! I am a good cleaner; I just hate to do it. I like organization and no clutter.

TOTAL NUMBER OF DAYS SPENT IN A DUCK BLIND: Two, but more to come. I really like hunting. I grew up going with my dad, but it's hard to go when you have four babies all two years apart.

BEST ADVICE ANYONE EVER GAVE ME: "Keep God first."

WORST ADVICE ANYONE EVER GAVE ME: "God would never want you to be unhappy."

MY MOTHER ALWAYS SAID: "Be nice to everyone, no matter where they come from, how much money they have, or the color of their skin."

I WOULD NEVER LEAVE THE HOUSE WITHOUT: My lipstick or ChapStick

MY FAVORITE THING TO DO DURING DUCK SEASON IS: Plan for Christmas

IF I COULD DO ONE THING TO CHANGE THE WORLD TODAY, I WOULD: Protect children from abusive situations

WHEN I WAS LITTLE, I WANTED TO GROW UP AND BE: An attorney. I now know I would have made a terrible lawyer.

Part One

HOW I BECAME A ROBERTSON

"Wherever you go, I will go; wherever you live, I will live. Your people will be my people, and your God will be my God. Wherever you die, I will die, and there I will be buried. May the Lord punish me severely if I allow anything but death to separate us!"

RUTH 1:16–17, NLT

INTRODUCTION

A Message from the Wives

All of us wives agree that being a Robertson is a privilege and a joy. We are a happy family; we love God, and we love each other. We help and support one another, and we each have a passion to see the others succeed. We work together, play together, pray together, and laugh together.

When people see us around the table at the end of each *Duck Dynasty* episode, they get a good glimpse into who we are because they can tell we are people of faith. But they do not get a complete picture of what makes our family work, and that is one reason we wrote this book.

We all came into the Robertson family the same way: we fell in love with a Robertson man and believed we could build a good life with him, a life based on faith and family. Of course, we also knew we might spend a good bit of time apart from him during duck season! We all value different aspects of the family and appreciate being part of this remarkable group for different reasons, but we all agree that our family is amazing and wonderful.

Miss Kay: I LOVED THEM BEFORE I KNEW THEM

For as long as I can remember, all I really wanted to do with my life was be the best wife and mother I could possibly be. As my boys began to grow up, I realized I also wanted to be the best mother-in-law I could be. Long before the boys met the women they eventually married, I began to pray for those girls. I prayed for them for years! I asked the Lord to give the boys godly wives who would love Him first and love them second. I don't believe any of my daughters-in-law ended up in the family by happenstance; God sent each one and each one is perfect for the Robertson man she married.

I believe the two most important decisions and vows we make are: first, to make Jesus Christ the Lord of our lives, and second, to choose godly mates and make lifelong commitments to them. I always knew the wives my sons chose would determine how their faith would grow and develop, and I prayed they would marry women who would help and encourage them spiritually. I am happy and thankful to say God has answered those prayers.

> For as long as I can remember, all I really wanted to do with my life was be the best wife and mother I could possibly be.
> —*Miss Kay*

Before my boys started dating, I made up my mind that I would love their wives. I never was one of those women who thought no young lady could be good enough for my son, and I never wanted to be a mother-in-law who competed with a daughter-in-law. I always had a heart to be kind and loving to whomever my sons chose, to be supportive of them and to embrace each one like my own daughter.

Lisa, Missy, Korie, and Jessica all know they can come to me for anything. If they have a fuss with their husbands, they know I will not automatically side with my boys. I will judge a situation according to what is right and wrong, based on what God says in His Word. I am not the kind of person who defends bad behavior just because one of my sons does it. If someone does something wrong, even if it's one of the boys, I will call it what it is!

I am glad to have such close relationships with my daughters-in-law and to be part of a great family of faith with them. Each one has a different personality and different ways of doing things. But each one is special to me and I love them all dearly!

Jessica: LET'S GET ONE THING STRAIGHT

Somehow, because of *Duck Dynasty*, people often brand us Robertson wives as "gold diggers." That might be offensive to us if we were thin-skinned or if it were true. But it is not. In fact, it's *so* not true that we always get a good laugh when we hear the latest rumor about how we married our husbands because of their fortunes. People know Miss Kay didn't marry Phil for his money, and they don't necessarily see Lisa as a gold digger because they know Alan worked for years as a pastor before joining Duck Commander. But Korie, Missy, and me—people seem to think we plotted and schemed to capture wealthy, long-haired hunters, determined to marry them for their riches. Let me set the record straight.

When Missy married Jase, hardly anyone outside the hunting world had ever heard of him. Missy worked full-time in an administrative role at a local medical clinic to help support the two of them. She never dreamed he would one day become duck call royalty!

Korie and Willie married while they were in college and they laugh now about having to go to a friend's house to do their laundry. They were on such a tight budget that their favorite mealtime splurge was chicken strips and macaroni and cheese out of a box. Willie has always been an industrious person and a hard worker. All of his life, he has been happy to pick up odd jobs for extra money, but in the early years of his and Korie's marriage, they were both in college and money was tight. When their children were young, Korie worked in a paid position as children's minister at our church. She also used her skills as a fine artist to paint detailed pictures on duck calls and sold them at hunting shows.

When I married Jep and for several years afterward, I had numerous jobs, including making hand-sewn heirloom dresses and smocked children's clothes to sell to boutiques, working as a Realtor, and being a sales representative for a clothing company. Though Jep has always been the head of our home and the leader of our family, I have always tried to contribute financially as best I could. When we first got married, several years before *Duck Dynasty* started, we lived in a little trailer and could barely make ends meet. We just wanted to be able to pay our bills, buy groceries, and put gas in our cars.

I can say with complete confidence that each one of us wives married her husband because she loved and respected him; we knew they were men we could honor and trust. All of us value and appreciate these men because of who they are on the inside, not because they are now TV stars. We all married them when they had very little, and we were happy. We struggled financially, just as many other couples do—and we were happy. Now God has blessed us with more resources than we have ever had, and we're still happy. But I can assure you that all of us would rather have strong, solid marriages with godly men than have all the riches this world could offer. And you can take *that* to the bank!

> We all married our Robertson men when they had very little, and we were happy. Now God has blessed us with more resources than we have ever had, and we're still happy. —*Jessica*

2

THE CHEERLEADER

AND THE QUARTERBACK

Miss Kay

I cannot remember a time in my life when I did not want to grow up, get married, and raise a family. I can remember a couple of times when I wanted to be an airline stewardess or a teacher, but those did not last very long. Being a wife and mother was always my dream, and it was never far from my mind. As I mentioned earlier, I not only wanted to be a wife and mother, I wanted to be *the best* wife and mother on earth. I believed that if I could do that, I would have a happy family and a great life.

As a child, the best role models I had were my grandparents. I loved my mom and dad, too, but my mother did some strange things I later found out were due to alcohol use, and my father, whom I adored, died when I was only fourteen years old. Before he passed away, my parents ran the local store in our community, a business that was in our family for seventy-five years. Taking care of the store took most of their time, so I spent a lot of time either at the store visiting with customers or with my grandparents.

A POWERFUL INFLUENCE

My grandmother, whom I called Nannie, loved to tell me stories from the old days and had a powerful influence on me. She married at the age of fifteen. She went to school for a short time before she had to quit but learned a lot about life because she survived some very hard times. She was also a woman of wisdom, because she was a woman of great faith, and faith and wisdom usually go together. She was a great cook and spent a lot of time working in the kitchen, like many women of her generation—before microwaves and the other gadgets that make cooking easy these days. She had a big, full garden and taught me all about gardening. At her house I had the best time picking vegetables, shelling peas, and shucking corn with her in preparation for a meal. She seemed to be cooking all the time and taught me to cook at a young age. One of my very favorite ways to spend time with Nannie was to stay right beside her and cook with her. We developed a very strong bond in the kitchen together, whether I was helping her cook her daily meals for the workers at my parents' store or helping her prepare smaller meals for our family. I definitely got my now-famous kitchen abilities from my grandmother, and Phil says he will always love her for that!

One of my favorite things to do when I was young was to spend my evenings after supper sitting and talking with Nannie in the big swing that sat in her yard. We spent hours and hours just swaying back and forth, talking about all kinds of things and waving to every car that drove by. I have wonderful memories of those times.

I also remember watching Nannie and my grandfather together. In one room of their house were two maple rocking chairs with a gas heater between them, and they sat in those chairs every day as Nannie read the Bible to my grandfather. In their bedroom were two double beds with a nightstand between them. When I spent the night with my grandparents, I slept with Nannie while my grandfather slept in the other bed, which I guess he did every night. Even though they did not sleep in the same bed, they both reached out and held hands across the nightstand, and I always thought that was so sweet. When we woke up the next morning, Nannie never failed to take my grandfather a cup of coffee, very early. That daily act of kindness touched me and I never forgot it. My grandmother had a true servant's heart, and she deeply loved her husband.

Because my grandmother was such an important part of my life and such a good example to me, her words carried a lot of weight. We never talked about anything intimate when it came to boys or men because people simply did not do that in her day, but she always told me that marriage is "one man, one wife—for life." I believed that as a child, and I still believe it today. I knew from a very young age that when I met the man I wanted to marry, I would stick with him!

A PERFECT MATCH

Phil says he and I have always been a perfect match. We started going together when I was in the ninth grade and he was in the tenth grade. He was the star quarterback of our high school football team, and I was a cheerleader. I was so happy to be dating him once we got together! We took a little break when hunting season started just after Christmas that year because Phil wanted to spend his free time hunting and decided he did not have time for a girlfriend. But then my dad died suddenly and Phil came to his funeral. I think he was trying to send the message that he cared about me—and it worked. I was glad he showed up, even though we did not have a chance to talk.

My dad had been my rock and my protector. I always felt safe with him and wanted to marry someone with qualities similar to his. I knew Phil was the same type of strong, protective person my dad was, so in many ways Phil became like a replacement for my dad. He gave me back some of what I lost when my dad passed away. In addition, he was everything I wanted in a man. I had always wanted someone outdoorsy and someone who was strong and cou-rageous. That was Phil!

A few weeks after my dad died, Phil asked me out and, of course, I went. We have basically been together ever since. My mother also started dating not too long after my dad passed away, so within several months of his death, she and I were both dating at the same time. That was not always good. I needed her help and guidance because I had not been in a relationship with a guy before, but she was not available. Plus, she was not in favor of my dating Phil because his family did not have much money. That was a lot more important to her than it was to me. During that time, I spent less time at home with my mother and more time at the Robertsons' house, surrounded by a happy, loving family.

As Phil and I grew closer, we faced the same temptations most young people deal with when they are in love. I did not know how to handle those feelings. My mother was not available to talk to and I felt I could not mention something like sex to my grandmother. I had always been a "good" girl. I was not the slightest bit adventurous as a child. I obeyed and I behaved. As a teenager I had to figure out a lot of things for myself. I was on my own when it came to knowing what to do about a physical relationship with Phil.

I always believed people should only sleep with one person, and I knew I wanted to marry Phil someday, so he would be that person for me. We did have sex before we got married and I did get pregnant. I know that these days, with *Duck Dynasty* on TV, some people think Phil and I are way too open about our sex life. In fact, some people in our own family are still shocked by the way we talk about it! I just have two things to say about that. First, we're married, and married people have sex. Second, I wish someone had been open with me and talked about sex when I was dating Phil. I desperately needed somebody to teach me what it was all about and help me understand how to deal with my young, intense feelings for him.

> **I needed my mother's help and guidance because I had not been in a relationship with a guy before, but she was not available.**
>
> —*Miss Kay*

A Whole New Life

When Phil graduated high school, he received a football scholar-ship to Louisiana Tech University. I was pregnant with Alan, so of course I went to Ruston, Louisiana, with Phil and we began our lives together in a little student-housing apartment. During our first year together I finished high school and had a baby, while Phil impressed coaches, players, and fans with his talents on the football field and went hunting in his spare time.

That was just the beginning of my life as part of the Robertson family. In a later chapter, I will write about some of the challenges Phil and I faced and about how we got through them. As of this writing, Phil and I have now been married nearly fifty years. I'm still in love with him, and I cannot imagine being part of any other family.

3

IT STARTED WITH A CRUSH

Lisa

In 1977, when I was in sixth grade at Pinecrest Elementary School in my hometown of West Monroe, Louisiana, I saw the cutest boy I had ever laid eyes on. He was new to our school, and I quickly found out his name was Alan Robertson. I was popular in school and people seemed to like me, but no matter how I tried, that cute boy did not seem to know I was alive. Maybe that's because he was in eighth grade and did not have time for younger girls like me. That did not stop me from following him around school, though—during every recess, fire drill, and class change. Sometimes when I speak publicly about this now, I say I could have been on fire and he would not have noticed. At least that's what I thought; he says he was vaguely aware that he had a sixth-grade stalker with braces.

By the end of that school year, Alan had become a favorite among his peers. He was even elected "Mr. Pinecrest," which he says is the only title he has ever really held. Because our school only went to eighth grade, I knew Alan would not be at Pinecrest the following year. Our paths did not cross again until he was the cool senior at our local high school and I was "kid" sophomore.

Not What I Expected

I was excited to see Alan again when I got to high school but soon realized he was not the same "nice boy" I remembered. He was spending time with one of my cousins, drinking and smoking pot on a regular basis. Many of the teenagers in our community often hung out at our local McDonald's, and Alan happened to notice me there one night. He thought I was attractive (actually, he says he thought I was a *babe*), so right then and there he asked me out for the following weekend.

I had been dreaming of a date with Alan Robertson since sixth grade. When I finally went out with him for the first time, it was horrible! He did not pick me up; he asked me to meet him. When he showed up, he had two of my cousins with him. Who wants to go on a date with their cousins? Our evening consisted of nothing more than cruising around in a car while my cousins got drunk and high. At the end of the date, even Alan was completely passed out. He did not turn out to be the gentleman I was hoping for, at least not that night.

People might think I would drop a guy who acted that way like a hot rock, but I did not. I kept seeing him and soon began

> I had been dreaming of a date with Alan Robertson since sixth grade. When I finally went out with him for the first time, it was horrible!
>
> —*Lisa*

smoking and drinking with him. I really cared about him and was willing to do anything to please him. When I say "anything," I mean *anything*.

Since Alan was such a looker, girls were always interested in him. I decided to make sure none of those girls got their meat hooks into the man I had been dreaming of. (I have a lot more redneck in me than my sisters-in-law. They are far more like "yuppie girls," as Phil would say.) On one occasion, one of Alan's former girlfriends tried to make her move on him and I had to show her how a country girl hangs on to her man! We had a good "cussin' catfight," and even though I was pretty scrawny back then, I held my own and neutralized the threat. I think Alan was impressed, and we laugh about it to this day. I learned way back then that someone or something you really care about is worth fighting for.

WHAT? YOU'RE *LEAVING*?

With Alan, I really thought I was in dating heaven. I was finally in a relationship with the man I had loved since sixth grade. I knew the way we were living was not the way love was supposed to go, but the fact that we were intimate convinced me we could be "in love" forever, no matter what happened—and things were definitely happening. Alan's behavior had deteriorated to the point that Phil and Miss Kay kicked him out of their house. He decided to go live with his aunt, Phil's sister, in New Orleans, a city that probably did not provide the atmosphere Phil and Miss Kay were hoping for. I hated to see him leave but truly believed our "love" could stand the long-distance test. After all, I loved him and had given myself to him. Surely that meant as much to him as it meant to me.

Alan now says he had no intention of continuing his relationship with me once he got to New Orleans. He also freely admits he did not have the character or integrity to inform me of that decision. All I knew was that I loved him, I missed him, and with every passing week, I was having a harder time reaching him by phone.

One weekend I finally decided to go with the Robertsons to visit Alan. He knew we were coming, so I was shocked when we arrived and discovered he was out on a date with someone else. That was his way of breaking up with me. I was devastated! I cried the whole way home from New Orleans to West Monroe and for a week after that.

ALAN COMES HOME

My broken heart sent me into a complete free fall. For the next year and a half I dedicated my life to finding the love I had lost with Alan. My life was a complete disaster. Alan's life in New Orleans was also a mess until he finally had an epiphany on the wrong end of a jealous husband's crowbar (Phil tells that story in detail in his book, *Happy, Happy, Happy*). After that incident, Alan came home to West Monroe and called me, and we went out again, this time under much better circumstances.

We knew that resisting the temptation to be physically intimate would be a problem while we were dating, so after we had dated about six months, Alan asked me to marry him. I was so happy! Of course, I said yes. He did not believe in long engagements so we were married the following Friday. This was not met with enthusiasm on my parents' part, but Alan and I were determined to begin our lives together immediately.

When we first married, we moved in with Phil's parents, Granny and Pa, who lived in a small house next door to Phil and Kay's larger house—not like typical next-door neighbors, but in a small house on Phil and Miss Kay's property, just down the hill from them. After about six months, Alan and I were able to buy a little camp house beside Miss Kay and Phil. I enjoyed being around them, and around Granny and Pa. I learned so much in those early years from these godly people—including how to cook, from none other than the kitchen commander herself, Miss Kay! Alan was long-suffering with me as I learned the ways of his mother's cooking, but in the end it paid off. I can cook most of what Miss Kay does and Alan will go so far as to say that some of my cooking is better than Miss Kay's, if you want to believe that.

My journey with Alan, and Alan's journey with me, has not been easy. It has not even been pretty at times. But we have learned to love God and to love each other, in that order. Being a Robertson has been a blessing to me for many years. I will always thank God for the chance to be Alan's wife and to be part of such a loving, supportive, forgiving family.

4

THE BEST JOKE I EVER PLAYED

Missy

I was sixteen and Jason (known on TV as Jase) was eighteen when we started dating. One of my friends—we'll call her Christy—was actually interested in him, and the two of them had started seeing each other. Jase did not know Christy was already dating someone else and had been for quite some time. He found this out at her house one Sunday afternoon when she ran down the stairs telling him he had to leave immediately. About that time, he heard the screeching of tires from the front of her house. Her boyfriend had arrived. The boyfriend (we'll call him Greg) was obviously not happy with the current arrangement and was there to set things straight with Jason. He told Jason he wanted to talk inside his truck. Jase ended up getting into Greg's vehicle, which he quickly regretted, and Greg proceeded to drive to an undisclosed location to fight it out. Quickly, Jase realized the situation and told Greg that if all of this was over Christy, he could have her. She was not worth it to him.

Since Greg did not seem to respond to this direction in the conversation, Jase switched gears and started preaching to him. He proceeded to tell Greg that Jesus died for him and for all the rotten things he had done in his life. He told him God would forgive him if he would turn his life over to Jesus, be baptized for his sins, and start living a life that reflected Jesus' love for him.

Since Greg did not seem to respond to this dialogue either, Jase told him simply, "Just don't hit me in the face." Greg stopped the truck, dragged Jase out, roughed him up a bit, and left him at the end of a dead-end road. Jason never threw one punch. Obviously, the relationship between Jason and Christy was officially over.

> **Since Greg did not seem to respond to this dialogue either, Jase told him simply, "Just don't hit me in the face."** —*Missy*

WE THOUGHT IT WAS JUST FOR FUN

News of what happened between Jason and Greg quickly hit our church youth group as well as Christy's and my friends at school. Jason and I started talking about the situation and, as a ruse, decided to go on a mock date with each other in order to make Christy jealous. (Remember, we were sixteen and eighteen at the time—not the most mature individuals.) I took him as my date to a school function, even though he had already graduated from another area school, to make sure Christy saw us together. We made sure she witnessed the fun we were having talking and laughing and flirting. I soon realized we really were talking, laughing, and flirting with each other, and I did not want the night to end. At some point during the evening, I think we both forgot about Christy. We actually have not thought much about her since.

I must share one more aspect of this story before I continue with what happened with Jase and me. A week after our date, during Sunday morning church services, someone tapped Jason on the shoulder and told him to look in the back of the auditorium. He turned around and saw Greg standing there. He thought, *Oh no, round two!* After services concluded, Greg approached Jase and told him that he actually listened when Jase was telling him about Jesus' love for him. He asked Jase to tell him again about Jesus and why He had died for him. He apologized to Jason for the one-sided fight and asked for his forgiveness. After hearing the message of Jesus again from the youth director, Greg was baptized that night. Today, Greg is a pilot with his own plane and has recently flown Jase and me to events where Jase shares that same message of Christ with many audiences.

THINGS GET SERIOUS

Now back to my story about how Jase and I ended up together. We started dating in the fall of 1987. Our first kiss was October 8, 1987. At first I was drawn to Jase because of his good looks, of course, but I soon noticed how self-confident he was. Not cocky, but self-confident; there is a big difference. He was not like any other boys I had dated, who tried to look and act cool in front of their friends. You know, those boys who would call and talk to you on the phone for hours one evening and then act like they did not know you in front of their friends the next day at school. I liked the fact that he was not that way.

My friends were not convinced Jason was right for me. I mean, he was a redneck from West Monroe, for goodness' sakes! I was a student at a private school in Monroe. Some of my friends were very well-off in terms of money and material possessions. They drove nice cars, lived in manicured neighborhoods, and, well, they didn't shoot their dinner!

Jason's family had nothing in common with my friends' families. The Robertsons had multiple cars, but he had to take a gamble on which one would work when he needed to drive. They had a basketball hoop nailed to a tree in their front yard, so there was absolutely no grass. Since they did not have a concrete driveway, they just pulled the vehicles up "in the yard," as they said. Their house was a two-bedroom, one-bath camp house with a laundry room addition and a metal roof off the back. It was twenty miles outside of town, in the middle of nowhere. And it was the busiest home I had ever seen in my life. The smells that came from that tiny kitchen were to die for! Miss Kay's corn bread and banana pudding were some of the first things I remember eating in that house.

The family welcomed me just like they welcomed every other soul who made the drive up "in the yard." They treated everybody the same, no matter how much money they had (or did not have), no matter what color skin they had, no matter who they voted for for president, and no matter what god they served. Everybody was welcome, and everybody was going to hear about Jesus from Phil. That family was like a magnet. They attracted any and all, and people found it very hard to tear themselves away.

Jason was true to who he was and what he believed. I was hooked immediately. The more we dated, the more I realized he could help me get to heaven. He was funny, confident, smart, driven, and super cute. We dated for a year and two months before he asked me to marry him. It went something like this.

It was Christmas of 1988, and we were exchanging our Christmas gifts alone at his grandparents' house, next to the family home. I gave him his gifts: an LSU sweatshirt and cap. And he gave me his gift: a small potted plant. When I gave him a look that said, "Are you kidding me?" he grinned and told me to dig in the dirt. Reluctantly, I dug into the little clay pot until I hit something. I uncovered a little felt box, pulled it out, and opened it to find a beautiful engagement ring! I looked at Jase with eyes wide, and he said words I will never forget: "Well, you're gonna marry me, aren't ya?" Obviously, I said yes. And that's my engagement story.

ONLY GOD COULD LOVE HIM MORE

Jason and I were married August 10, 1990, in our home church, the same church we still attend together with all our family. Our wedding was completely perfect. My parents did not have much money (my dad is a preacher, and my mom was a teacher at our private Christian school). My dress was the exact duplicate of a beautiful gown I had spotted in our local bridal store, thanks to my mom's best friend, who was a wonderful seamstress. It had all the details of the designer gown: beads, lace, tulle, and more. It also had big puffy sleeves—it was the end of the eighties era, you know. I sang a song entitled "Only God Could Love You More," which I prerecorded and played as I walked down the aisle. That song title was exactly how I felt about Jase, and I knew he felt the same way about me.

Oh, remember Christy? Her dad was our preacher at the time, and he officiated the wedding. Needless to say, we were all back to being friends. All of Jase's brothers were in our wedding, as well as Lisa, Alan's wife. I was the second woman Jase's family brought into the Robertson fold. I was nineteen.

5

YOUNG LOVE

Korie

The first time I met Phil, he asked a friend and me, "Have you girls met my sons Jason Silas and Willie Jess?"

We nervously answered, "Yes, sir."

Then he went on to say, "They'll make good husbands someday."

Keep in mind, my friend and I were only in the fifth grade when this conversation happened. He went on to tell us that his sons would be good providers because they were good hunters and fishermen. This did not really matter to me at the time; I just thought Willie was cute.

Now, I have to tell you, Phil is a little intimidating when you first meet him, so this was all a little embarrassing and shocking to me. Before this meeting, I had only been around Willie one other time. Let me explain.

WORTH WRITING ABOUT

As a child, one of the highlights of my year was going to summer camp. When I was in the third grade, my whole life changed at that camp, though I did not know it at the time. There, as an eight-year-old girl, I had my first crush—on the person who would eventually become my husband.

I fell for Willie immediately. In all my young life I had never seen such cute dimples and such a great smile. I was smitten. Like a lot of girls my age I had a diary, but I did not write in it much. But Willie was worth an entry, which read: "I met a boy at summer camp and he was so cute. He asked me on the moonlight hike, and I said yes!"

Each year at our camp, the girls wondered which young man would ask them to walk with him on the hike. There was only one boy I wanted to go with, and I was thrilled when he asked me. If a moonlight hike at summer camp counts as a date, then Willie and I had our first date that year and it was a success!

> **Willie was worth a diary entry, which read: "I met a boy at summer camp and he was so cute. He asked me on the moonlight hike, and I said yes!" —*Korie***

Even though Willie and I lived in the same fairly small city, we did not see each other for quite some time after camp that summer. We did not attend the same school, nor did our families go to the same church. The Robertsons went to a small country church, while my family worshipped at White's Ferry Road Church.

I NEVER FORGOT HIM

I ended up at Phil and Miss Kay's house a few years later because I was friends with the daughter of the preacher at our church. Her name was Rachel. Her father had struck up a friendship with Phil and was trying to convince him to bring his family to White's Ferry Road. I was beyond excited when Rachel asked me to join her family at a fish fry at the Robertsons' house so the families could get to know each other and the Robertsons could learn more about the church. Even though I had not seen Willie in two years, I had not forgotten him.

When we arrived at the Robertsons', I was nervous, but I remember a lot about that night. Strangely, I can still picture exactly what I was wearing. It was the eighties, so of course my jeans were tight-rolled, and I wore a black waffle-weave shirt with a fluorescent-green rope belt and fluorescent-pink dangly earrings. I also remember thinking Willie was the funniest guy I had ever met. He worked hard to impress me by blowing on his thumb and blowing up his muscle, and showing me all his "Vulcan death grips." In addition to those things, he ate sardines straight out of a can. This was all pretty impressive to a ten-year-old!

Two things about that visit to Willie's house caught my attention. First was the fact that Phil told me what a good husband he would be as soon as I walked in the door. Second was that Phil and Miss Kay had a sign on their bedroom door that read HONEYMOON SUITE. Of course I did not say anything, but even then I was surprised at how blatant they were about their honeymooning. Now, because of *Duck Dynasty*, millions of people know that Phil and Kay freely discuss that aspect of their lives.

After that night, I did not see Willie again for another two years. Seeing the guy who had captured my heart once every two years was hard on my love-struck young self. Thankfully, the Robertsons finally joined our church when I was in seventh grade. All the girls were immediately interested in Jase and Willie, not only because they were new but also because they were good-looking and they were genuinely nice guys.

Willie finally asked me out on our first real date—if we don't count the moonlight hike—when I was in the eleventh grade. At that time, because he had not been nice to one of my friends a few years earlier, I didn't go out with him. She had given him money to buy her a soft drink on a church trip, and he bought baseball cards instead. Of all the nerve! Willie went on to date other people and so did I.

Not long after Christmas during my senior year in high school, in 1990, Willie and I saw each other at the mall. Without ever saying anything, we both seemed to know we would see each other again. Things had changed. I called him a couple of days later, knowing I needed to be the one to reach out to him since I was the one who had rejected him previously. I had to leave a message for him and was thrilled when he returned my call the next day. We went to lunch at Bonanza that day, and by the end of January 1991, we were definitely dating. And we were serious.

I WASN'T GOING TO MISS THIS OPPORTUNITY

In the fall of 1991, I was preparing to go to college at Harding University in Searcy, Arkansas. I was hoping to convince Willie to join me, but he was attending seminary school at our church and was not the least bit interested in going to college or leaving West Monroe. He did not want me to go either, but I had wanted to go to Harding since I was a little girl. Both my parents had gone there, and I had an academic scholarship. This was a tough decision, but I decided it was an opportunity I did not want to pass up, so Willie and I broke up before I left for school.

A few weeks later, in September, Willie called me and said he wanted to get back together. I knew in my heart that I loved him and wanted to get back together, too, but I was not quite ready to tell him, so I said I would call him back the next day. When I did, I simply said, "Let's get back together." That was the last time we ever broke up. About a month later, we decided we were ready to get married.

My engagement to Willie did not go over well with my parents. They had nothing against Willie, but they had a *lot* against our getting married so young. I was barely eighteen! A huge argument between Willie and my parents, complete with shouting on both sides, took place at Alan and Lisa's house, where Willie was living at the time.

My parents are not yellers. I actually do not remember an argument like that with my parents before or since that night. I am glad I wasn't there to witness it, but I realize that tempers were high because everyone involved really loved me and wanted the best for me. They simply did not agree on what "the best" was.

The argument did not end well. Willie called to tell me just how badly it went. And then something surprising happened: My parents called me and said, "If you're determined to do this, we're going to support you." I was, they did, and they've never stopped.

My parents threw Willie and me a big, beautiful wedding on January 11, 1992. We had ice sculptures and white trees, which made the place look like a winter wonderland. Since Willie and I were both born and raised in the West Monroe area, lots of family and friends came to our wedding—about eight hundred of them. It was such a happy time. And it was enough of a big deal to Phil that he wore his dress-up clothes: corduroy pants and a button-down shirt!

Adventurous Beginnings

Willie did end up moving to Searcy, Arkansas, with me. In fact, we moved the day after we got married and settled into a tiny one-bedroom apartment. Not long after that, with my parents' help, we bought a very small house where we lived while going to school at Harding. We were on a super-tight budget, and some of our biggest fights happened at the grocery store when we had a few extra dollars and I wanted to buy a *People* magazine while Willie wanted to buy baseball cards. We certainly could not afford both.

One of the great opportunities Willie and I had during college was the chance to spend a summer in Florence, Italy. This was part of a study-abroad program, and we were so excited. We had never been away from home together until we took that trip. As I mentioned, we moved to Arkansas immediately after our wedding, so we did not take a honeymoon trip. My parents did take us to Hawaii the following summer, and we all had a wonderful time, but it was more of a family vacation than a romantic getaway.

Willie and I had all kinds of new and exciting experiences in Italy. We wanted to see Europe, but we did not have money for hotel rooms, so we traveled by train at night from one country to another. We boarded the train in one country, went to sleep, and woke up somewhere else. We had all kinds of adventures in Italy and in various other European countries. We were glad to get home when we returned to the States that fall, but we were also happy and grateful for all the fun we had and for everything we learned while we were away.

I was born into a wonderful, godly family, and I am so blessed to have also become a Robertson. Phil was exactly right when he told me many years ago that Willie would make a good husband. Willie's a great husband and father, and I am so glad I married him. I love being his wife, and I love being part of such a fun and loving family—but I still find myself surprised at times when Phil and Kay talk as openly as they do about their honeymooning!

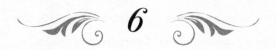

6

FANCY MEETING YOU HERE

Jessica

I first met the man I married at a hair salon. I was going out the door; Jep was going in—for a haircut. Seriously. Nowadays, most of the Robertson men don't get haircuts, but Jep did back then. When our paths crossed that day, we said nothing more than "hi" to each other, just one word.

Jep and I both grew up in West Monroe, Louisiana, and he is two years older than I am. We went to different high schools, but because we lived in a close community, we had heard about each other. He knew who I was, and I knew who he was—and I thought he had a cool name. I had heard good things about him, including, "He's a dream." When our paths crossed at the hair salon and we simply said hello, I had no way of knowing the hairdresser would tell Jep all about me as she cut his hair that day. Both of us had gone to her for years, so she knew us pretty well, and she said really nice things about me to Jep. In fact, she takes credit for getting us together! After we were married I found out that when he left the hair salon that day, he went home and told his best friend, "I just met the girl I'm going to marry."

"What's her name?" his friend asked.

"Jessica," Jep responded. He only knew this because the hairdresser had told him.

"Jessica who?" his friend asked. "What's her last name?"

"I don't know," Jep admitted.

I love the fact that Jep knew he would marry me after only seeing me once. Maybe he did not know my last name, but the next time he saw me, he made sure to find out a little more about me.

WHAT EXACTLY *IS* A DUCK COMMANDER?

A few weeks after our encounter at the hair salon, Jep and I both attended a concert in our hometown and saw each other again. He walked up to me and said, "I'm Jeptha Robertson. You're Jessica, right?"

We went on to have a conversation that went something like this.

Jep said, "My dad is Phil Robertson."

I was unimpressed. Even though I come from a family of hunters, I had never heard of Phil Robertson, and that seemed obvious to Jep, so he continued. "You know, the Duck Commander."

I'd heard of Daffy Duck; Donald Duck; and Duck, Duck Goose, but I had never heard of a Duck Commander. "What is a duck commander?" I asked, not sure if it would be a person, a job title, a tool, or what.

Jep was totally shocked by my ignorance but very sweet about it. I thought his disbelief was cute. Our interaction did not go much further beyond the fact that I did not know who Phil was, but it was pleasant.

The next time I saw Jep was at a Chili's restaurant. He was there with his friends and I was there with my family. He and his friends were going home, to a house he rented with one of his buddies, to play a game of dominoes. Jep invited me to join them. At that time, I was a homebody and an introvert. I was not adventurous in any way and felt uneasy about playing games with people I did not really know. But there was just something intriguing about Jep that caused me to step out of my comfort zone and go with Jep and his buddies.

> I'd heard of Daffy Duck; Donald Duck; and Duck, Duck Goose, but I had never heard of a Duck Commander. —*Jessica*

Not long after the night we first played dominoes, Jep invited me to a Bible study he held with his friends several nights a week. Those guys preached the Gospel to me, and soon after I started attending the study, Jep baptized me one night in a muddy pond in a local neighborhood. By the time we got there, it was already dark, so we used Jep's Jeep headlights to help us see so we could wade in and out of the water.

MEETING THE ROBERTSONS

Soon after Jep baptized me, I met his family. I have always thought of myself as an old soul, and I felt an immediate connection with Miss Kay. From the time we met, we have been close. That's my perspective of course, but if you ask her, she will tell you the same thing!

Jep, too, has always been close to his mom. After we married she told me that when we were dating, but before I met her, she asked him one day why he liked me so much and why he thought I was the one for him. I have always thought his answer was so sweet. He said to her, "Momma, of all the girls I've dated, this one is the most like you."

In June 2000, Jep and I admitted we really liked each other and began dating. In September, we broke up. I was miserable without Jep, and I think he was miserable without me. We finally said to each other, "I missed you," and got back together after only a couple of weeks apart. Later that month, we were studying the Bible together one evening at Phil and Miss Kay's house and Jep said, "We should get married." There was no getting down on one knee, no long profession of his undying love for me, just that matter-of-fact observation. I knew by that time that God had brought us together for a reason and that Jep loved me and would love me forever, so I did not need any of that; I simply agreed: yes, we should get married.

Joining the Family

On Sunday, October 7, 2001, just two weeks after Jep and I agreed to marry, we had a beautiful wedding in the backyard of a family friend. It was just what we wanted—outside on a gorgeous fall day, surrounded by nature and people we loved. Alan performed the ceremony, and Missy, a talented vocalist, sang. It was not elaborate because we did not have time to plan a big wedding. It all happened quickly, but it was perfect in our eyes.

The day we married we went to church in the morning, then Jep told me he needed to go somewhere and would see me later. I had no idea what he was going to do but found out he went straight from church to the mall, which opened at noon, to buy me a ring. I now know Miss Kay had also bought me a ring, at Walmart I think, because she wanted to make sure I had one and knew Jep did not have much money. I will always be grateful to her for being so thoughtful about that. But it was important to Jep to buy me a ring himself, so he picked a simple, pretty wedding band out and paid for it over time. It's the ring I still wear with love and pride. No big diamond necessary! By two o'clock that afternoon, I was wearing a dress I had bought off the sale rack at Dillard's and Jep was wearing a borrowed outfit consisting of a pair of slacks, a button-down shirt that was slightly large, and a tie. Both of us were ready to commit the rest of our lives to each other.

One thing I noticed early on about Jep—and part of what made me fall in love with him—is that he is so kind, generous, and eager to help anyone. When I became part of the Robertson family, I quickly realized one thing about them: Robertsons are some of the most loving people I have ever known. They have open doors and open arms to everyone. Phil and Miss Kay are incredibly generous people, and the rest of the family has followed their example. In fact, I would go so far as to say that part of what it means to be a Robertson is to love and serve others, no matter their background, skin color, or status in life. I can remember times when Phil and Kay had nothing to offer financially, but they shared their love and faith with everyone. They have always helped anyone they can, in any way they can. When I think of becoming a Robertson, it has meant so much more to me and to all the wives than simply a change of last name. When we became part of the family, we became part of everything Phil and Kay represent and taught their sons to represent. I am so thankful to belong to a family so deeply rooted in love for God and love for others.

Part Two

NO ORDINARY IN-LAWS

Two people are better off than one, for they can help each other succeed.

ECCLESIASTES 4:9, NLT

INTRODUCTION

A Message from the Daughters-in-Law

Missy's first visit to the Robertson home took place as a teenager when she went to their house for a Sunday night church group meeting. She remembers that when she got there, she said to herself, "These people are different from anyone I've ever met." A lot of people would probably say the same about Miss Kay and Phil. They *are* different from anyone most of us encounter on a regular basis, and they are different in all the best ways. Not much about them is ordinary, and they certainly do not fit the traditional stereotypes of in-laws. We could not be happier about that, and we could not love and appreciate them any more than we do. They are extraordinary individuals and extraordinary in-laws.

> Not much about Phil and Miss Kay is ordinary, and they certainly do not fit the traditional stereotypes of in-laws.

8

OH, KAY!

A Message from the Daughters-in-Law

As Miss Kay's daughters-in-law, we feel blessed with the best mother-in-law on earth. She means something different to each of us, and we enjoy our own special relationships with her. But we all immediately respond with some of the same answers when people ask us about her. We say she is an absolute joy to be around and that she is one of the most fun people we know. And we tell them that none of us feels like an in-law; she loves each one of us as she loves her own children.

We have all had experiences when we turned to her for good advice during disagreements with our husbands, and we've learned to trust her to be fair and objective, never taking the boys' side just because they are her sons. She is not quick to find fault with anyone but listens to all sides of a situation and judges it based on what is right or wrong according to God's Word. She will tell us—or the guys—when we are wrong. We can count on her for wisdom, comfort, encouragement, and a big dose of love. Most of all, Miss Kay has an enormous, forgiving heart. Years ago, that put our family on track to become who we are today and it remains part of what keeps us strong.

Missy: GREAT MOTHER-IN-LAW, GREAT FRIEND

Miss Kay is a great mother-in-law because she is a great friend. I don't think of her as my mother-in-law first. She is a friend first whom I am fortunate to have as my husband's mother. When I am with girlfriends and the subject turns to mother-in-law problems, which it sometimes does, I sit very quietly. I honestly have nothing to contribute. I hear my friends talk about how their mothers-in-law try to control them, try to tell them how to parent their kids, make snide comments about their choices of clothes, and so forth. I do not have any of those experiences with Kay, and usually, before the conversation is over, someone makes a comment about how I can't relate because I have Miss Kay as my mother-in-law. It is definitely apparent to everyone that I have the best mother-in-law in the world. Bar none. I tend to agree.

I learned about 90 percent of what I know about cooking from watching Kay. At my wedding shower, I received a recipe card set. I took that set of blank cards and headed straight for Miss Kay's kitchen. I pulled them out, took the first one, got a pen, and asked her to start giving me recipes for the things Jase liked to eat best. She happily obliged.

There was only one problem. Miss Kay had no idea what any measurement was for any of her ingredients. She would say, "One shake of this," or "Two scoops of that." Since I had no knowledge of cooking, I was looking for exact measurements. I did not want to mess up Jase's favorite recipes. I had some big shoes to fill, for goodness' sake!

Miss Kay tried to give me her best directions while she was busy around the house. At that time she didn't understand how little I knew, and we both became frustrated. One example of this was when she told me how to make mashed potatoes. She said to cut up four or five large potatoes and boil them. I asked, "How long do you boil them?"

She replied, "Until they're done."

"How many minutes does that take?" I asked, thinking I could set a timer.

She said, "You can't go by time."

"Then how do you know when they're done?"

"They're done when they're soft," she answered.

Thinking about how much I did not want to stick my hands in boiling water to see when they turned soft, I asked, "How do you know when they are soft?"

At that point, Miss Kay had become completely frustrated at this whole ridiculous line of questioning on my part. She said rather abruptly, "You stick a fork in them!"

I apologized for my ignorance, and Miss Kay realized I needed special attention. She then pulled up a chair, put her hand on my arm, and said, "Okay, let's start from the beginning." The next few minutes consisted of her gently instructing me in the ways of heating canned corn in a skillet, browning hamburger meat for her homemade spaghetti, making her famous homemade white sauce, and creating many other dishes I still make for my family on an almost daily basis.

One of my most special memories of Miss Kay is what she did when we found out our daughter, Mia, would be born with special needs. Miss Kay bought a new white baby bed (Mia was the first girl in the family for Jase and me), lots of antique knickknacks, and a beautiful antique baby doll carriage for her room. Jase and I did not have much extra money back then for a baby room makeover and neither did Phil and Miss Kay, so she also helped arrange the make-over as a surprise for me.

I worked at Duck Commander at that time, and the company was still run out of Phil and Miss Kay's house, so she distracted me by keeping me busy at work until late in the day. I came home to a completely redone baby room for my daughter. Jason's cousin Melissa, Korie, and some of my friends had spent the entire day getting it ready. It was absolutely beautiful, with mint-colored walls, white furniture (all of which I owned but had been repainted to match a girl's room), my great-great-grandmother's rocking chair reupholstered, new pink and white bedding, and even old children's books Kay found at garage sales. It was very emotional for me.

Miss Kay knew she could not change the outcome of this baby's being born with problems, so she did what she does best: she gave everything she could to provide comfort. I was so very proud of that room and, except for the baby bed, kept it exactly the same when we moved into the home we have now. I didn't change it until Mia's eighth birthday.

Lisa: A Friendship That Weathered the Storm

Miss Kay and I are only eighteen years apart, so even when I was a young newly married woman, she and I got along well. During those early years we developed a friendship that has stood the test of time and of great difficulty, a friendship that has survived what would have devastated many mother-in-law–daughter-in-law relationships. But Miss Kay is no ordinary mother-in-law, and the Robertson women as a whole are not ordinary women. We do fight for what we love and believe in. Miss Kay and I both believe a marriage is one of those relationships to love, to believe in, and to fight for, second only to a person's relationship with Christ.

When I first married Alan, I did not have a great relationship with my parents. They were not thrilled about my union with Alan. In their defense, I will say that way back then, he was not the fine upstanding man he is today. Miss Kay helped to mold me during those days, and I will be eternally grateful to her always for being there for me when I needed that guidance.

Kay's and my friendship just seems to thicken with time and with every obstacle Satan tries to use to knock us down. One of the things Kay and I try to do is to encourage our girls (my younger sisters-in-law) to face problems head-on. We have learned not to sweep problems under the rug because one day they will raise their ugly heads and take a bite out of you! I think when Kay and I work together like this, it makes our bond even stronger. I am truly a blessed woman to have the Robertson family, but I am doubly blessed to have a wise and loving woman like Kay as my mother-in-law.

As each daughter-in-law has joined our family, I have seen Kay work hard to establish a special relationship with her, just as each of her sons' wives has worked to build a special relationship with Miss Kay. She is not jealous of our relationships with her sons; she wants close relationships with us too. She knows that, down the road, interfering will only bring heartache for the ones she loves.

Miss Kay's best quality is her gentle, encouraging spirit. No matter what a person is going through, she will say she understands, but she is also quick to remind us that God can heal any situation and use it to His glory. I have learned from Miss Kay how important it is not to write people off just because they are dealing with a particular struggle. She has a remarkable ability to see the good in people and to give them opportunities to realize their potential. She definitely showed me how to believe in my children,

> Kay is not jealous of our relationships with her sons; she wants close relationships with us too. —*Lisa*

love them, and show them the way to the Lord even when I may not have agreed with their ways of thinking. Scripture tells us to train our children in the way of the Lord and that when they are older, they will not depart from it (Proverbs 22:6). Kay has lived that verse and made it part of her legacy to us.

Korie: SHE KEEPS THE FAMILY FUN

Miss Kay has such a fun spirit. She is lighthearted, she loves to laugh, and she has a great sense of humor. She looks for the fun in everything, and if she cannot readily find it, she makes it. Even as grown men, her sons can be very playful with her. They love to tickle her or walk up behind her in the kitchen and put an ice cube down the back of her shirt. She never gets upset with them, even if she is trying to get a meal on the table. In fact, she loves it! She thinks what they do is so cute and funny, and there's no doubt that her boys have inherited her playful spirit. She has fun with all of us and we have fun with her. *Duck Dynasty* shows the boys pulling pranks and being silly, and in real life, they do the same. Life around Miss Kay and her boys is lots of fun because Miss Kay is a fun person.

Miss Kay is also genuinely kind. One of the sweetest things she does for friends and family is send cards to them. Often she includes an encouraging note or some little message that really makes the recipient feel special. But other times, especially for our birthdays or other holidays, she gives us totally random cards, maybe because she likes the picture or the sentiment they express. Sometimes the sentiment doesn't even match the holiday or occasion! Getting a "Happy Valentine's Day" card in October with the word *Valentine's* scratched out and *Birthday* written over it is not uncommon. Miss Kay's philosophy is to buy the card she likes and then alter it to fit the celebration. No matter what the occasion, we all laugh at our mismatched cards.

Miss Kay has many "favorite" things, such as her dogs and her cookbooks, but there's not a doubt in anyone's mind that Miss Kay's pride and joy is her family. She loves it when we are all at her house, and she misses us when she does not see us for a couple of days. Miss Kay has spent her lifetime showing her love for others by cooking huge meals. But just as much as she loves the actual cooking, she loves her family being around her *while* she's cooking.

She makes everyone feel loved and important just for being in her home.

Since we began *Duck Dynasty*, all of our schedules have gotten incredibly busy, but Miss Kay is determined to continue her Bible-study groups and the many things she does to care for others. Many weeks, the ladies in the group have to change the time or the day of their Bible study to accommodate Miss Kay's filming schedule, but they love her so much they're willing to work it out. I really respect the fact that she doesn't choose to slow down when everyone would understand if she did. She is always thinking of what she can do to help someone else. I've seen her cook extra food for families who are in need. I've watched her stop just to buy a card for a friend who needed a word of encouragement. Between filming scenes for *Duck Dynasty*, I've even heard her on the phone counseling young women who are having marriage trouble. Miss Kay will do whatever it takes to help those she loves.

Miss Kay has taught me not to take my family or my marriage for granted. This is something anyone around her can see because she lives it every day. She works on her relationships. I don't think Miss Kay even realizes she is teaching this lesson because it comes so naturally to her, but I see how she does it. She continuously makes sure she gives her marriage the attention it needs to grow and thrive. She purposefully thinks about ways to make it better and to make Phil happy, happy, happy. She does the same for the rest of the family. She thinks of ways to bring us together and notices if one person needs a little more attention at a certain time or is struggling with something, and then she works to encourage the person or fix the problem. These valuable life lessons are now a part of my life, and I hope my children and husband can see me doing the same.

Jessica: THE BIGGEST HEART I KNOW

The first time I met Miss Kay, she gave me a big bear hug. Since that day, as long as I have known her, I have felt she embraced me as her very own, and the two of us have had a very strong relationship. When Jep and I first got together, I was the new girl at church dating a guy most girls thought was really good-looking (and he was). That is not usually a good way to make friends with other young women, so for quite a while I felt that Miss Kay was the only friend I had.

The fact that Miss Kay embraced me as she did is not really surprising. She has a bigger heart for people than anyone I have ever known. She is a friend to all—seriously, to everyone she meets. She picks up friends like nobody I have ever seen, but she also has a lot of long-standing relationships because she is so loyal to her friends. When you are Miss Kay's friend, it means that when you are discouraged or disappointed, she will help lift your spirits. When you are sad, she will comfort you. And when you make a mistake, she will never tear you down or try to make you feel bad about yourself.

Miss Kay is a pure delight to be around. She expresses her affection freely and has taught me by example so much about how to love and how to forgive. Jep and I did not date for very long before we married, so in many ways we had to learn about each other after our wedding. Miss Kay was so helpful and loving toward me during that time, as she helped me know how to be an encouraging and supportive wife. Those lessons helped me do my part to lay a firm foundation for a good marriage.

Kay and I were both blessed with very close relationships with our grandmothers. Her mother's mother, Nannie, had a major influence on her life and Miss Kay learned so much from her, especially about cooking. Kay loved her grandmother greatly and valued the things her grandmother told her. Likewise, I love my mamaw Nellie so much, and the two of us have had a strong bond with each other ever since I can remember. I still treasure the things she has said to me and the lessons she has taught me all these years. She is truly one of the most godly women I have ever known.

Miss Kay and I also have similar tastes. We both love classic movies, especially Doris Day movies and films like *Pride and Prejudice*. We also both enjoy old-timey music and have a love for hats. Some people even call us "the hat ladies." Miss Kay and I share an appreciation of antiques and have taken many girl trips to a well-known antiques area near Dallas, Texas. She and I do dinner-and-a-movie nights together and have been in many women's Bible-study groups with each other. Every time I am with her, I have fun and feel blessed to have her as my mother-in-law.

9

GETTING OUR PHIL

A Message from the Daughters-in-Law

One thing we can say with total confidence and unity about Phil is that he is a man of the Word—God's Word, that is. If there is anything he loves more than a good duck hunt, it is studying the Bible and sharing God's love with people. We honor him for the hard choices he has made in his life as he has chosen to follow God and for his steadfast, unshakable faith.

Phil is definitely not concerned about what other people think of him; he has very strong convictions and he lives his life according to them. Phil is a wise and loving man and a great leader in our family. We are thankful to have such a great father-in-law.

Korie: A WISE AND HUMBLE MAN

I know it won't be breaking news to anyone for me to say that Phil is blunt. He just "tells it like it is" all the time—no sugarcoating, no diplomacy, no punches pulled. But Phil is also incredibly wise. That catches some people by surprise, but everyone in our family recognizes and respects the wisdom in this man. In many ways, he has had a tough life and he has learned a lot through his experiences. Any time my children have a chance to be around him—whether it's in a duck blind or a fishing boat, out working on his land, or around the table—I want them to be.

One of the things I value most about Phil is his passion for God. He knows the Bible backward and forward. He was baptized almost forty years ago but still thirsts like a new Christian to learn and grow and share what God has done. He studies God's Word all the time; I don't know that he ever reads anything else.

Even though Phil is very wise, holds a master's degree, invented a famous duck call, and played some pretty good football in his day, he is also very humble. It would be easy for Phil, especially as he's gotten older, to sit back and rest on what he has accomplished in life, but he doesn't. He is always open to growing and changing and even to being proven wrong, if someone could do that. When he is not sure about something, he'll say, "Hey, why not? Let's try it." Not many men in Phil's position are willing to be challenged like he is.

Sometimes Phil can come across as hardheaded and intimidat-

> I know it won't be breaking news to anyone for me to say that Phil is blunt. —*Korie*

ing, and in some ways that might be true. But what many people don't realize about Phil is that he truly loves people. He really wants the best for them. That is his motivation for doing what he does, especially when it comes to sharing Jesus with others. His love for his fellow man drives him to open his home to complete strangers to tell them the good news of Jesus.

In many families, when control of a family business is passed from one generation to another, the older generation struggles to let go. That has never been the case with Phil. He has always shown respect and support for Willie as Willie has taken over the company his dad started and ran for many years. Again, this is a rare trait in someone with Phil's experience, but it sure has made Willie's job a *lot* easier!

Jessica: HE MAKES US WANT TO BE LIKE HIM

When I first had a chance to be around Phil, I thought he was rather quiet. The more time I spent in his presence, the more I realized he is a great storyteller, and he definitely has some great stories to tell. I also found out quickly that he is a man who truly loves God and is not afraid for anyone to know it. He genuinely cares about people's souls. He is so good at forgiving people and not holding anything against anyone.

I am so grateful for the way Phil understands and shows true forgiveness, because he taught Jep to do the same. When Jep and I first met, I was going through something a lot of twenty-year-olds go through. I had "baggage." Jep later told me that when he talked to Phil about it, Phil said, "Since she is a child of God Almighty, she is forgiven." He reminded Jep that my sins were washed clean by the blood of Christ.

I think Jep has always valued his parents' thoughts and opinions. He always took to heart the scripture "honor your father and mother" (Exodus 20:12). The fact that Phil spoke such affirming words to Jep about me gave him the courage to take the next step in our relationship. I will always appreciate that more than I can say.

A lot of parents tell their children and grandchildren, "Do as I say, not as I do." Phil never needs to say anything like that. He lives in such a way that he inspires us to want to do what he does. He "walks the walk"; he does not just "talk the talk." He is deeply committed to knowing God through His Word and when we look at Phil's life, we want to be the same way. His faithfulness and constant willingness to learn more about God have set an awesome example for all of our family.

Missy: HE'S HAPPY TO SHARE

To me, Phil's best quality is his love for the Lord and his thirst for the knowledge of God. When I picture Phil at home, I picture him laid back in his recliner with one leg over the arm of his chair, his reading glasses on, his Bible open, with a notebook and a pen on his lap. This is a scene I have witnessed too many times to count. Sometimes he acknowledges my presence, sometimes he doesn't, depending on how deep he is into his study. Matthew 5:6 describes Phil: "Blessed are those who hunger and thirst for righteousness, for they will be filled." He truly has a longing for God's Word, and he loves to share his knowledge whenever he gets a chance.

Phil has taught me to never judge a book by its cover. From the beginning of my relationship with Jase, I saw this firsthand in Phil. He accepted all people into his home. Everyone who entered his house got the same treatment. They were told about Jesus and asked how their lives were going. Some people were honest with Phil; some were dishonest. It didn't matter. Every person was treated like the one before and the one after. They got a meal, a bed (or couch) if needed, and a Bible study.

Phil does not get upset or excited about much. He does not get out of his chair to shake your hand if you are wealthy or famous, because he does not get out of his chair if you aren't. No one is better than anyone else in his eyes. Without Jesus, everyone is lost. That pretty much puts everyone on an even playing field. Phil looks at everyone the same way. His attitude is, "That person needs Jesus, and I am more than happy to share Him with them." I *love* that about Phil.

> **Phil has taught me to never judge a book by its cover.**
> —*Missy*

Lisa: STAND BY . . .

Phil has always been the big, burly, totally straightforward guy he is today. After all, he was once a star quarterback! Even with his imposing physical presence, I never had any reservations about speaking my mind in front of him or in front of Miss Kay. That was not always a good thing, but they understood my immaturity and did not keep a record of my wrongs.

One of the most important lessons I have learned in life I learned from Phil. It is this: whether or not you agree with a decision your child has made, you still stand by that child (even if he or she is an adult) and you stand by that decision.

When Alan and I had our relationship problems in the late 1990s (more about this later), Phil told Alan that he did not think we should get back together. Alan made the decision to accept me back into our home and into his life. When that happened, Phil told Alan that even though he thought I would just hurt him again, he would respect Alan's decision and he would treat me with respect. That is exactly what he has done since that time, and he has never once questioned our decision. He even defended Alan's choice when others questioned him and tried to put stipulations on the relationship. Phil has acted out 1 Corinthians 13:5, which says that love keeps no record of wrongs.

10

WHAT A TEAM!

A Message from the Daughters-in-Law

Sometimes people who have been married as long as Phil and Miss Kay reach a point where they lead comfortable but somewhat separate lives. This is definitely not true for Phil and Miss Kay. Although they are not "joined at the hip," and they do not do everything together every day (Miss Kay would not want to spend that much time in a duck blind), they have a great relationship and an exceptionally strong marriage. They know how to work together, play together, serve God together, and love our family together. They are both strong, gifted individuals, and they make a terrific team.

Jessica: WHO COULD ASK FOR ANYTHING MORE?

Growing up, my mother got along very well with my father's parents, and my father got along very well with hers. They both loved each other's families and enjoyed spending time with them. We spent many summers as a family at my dad's parents' fishing camp and many weekends and holidays during fall and winter hunting seasons at my mom's parents' hunting camp. Sometimes, both sets of grandparents ended up at the hunting camp, and all of us had a great time together.

People sometimes tell horror stories about their in-laws, but I never saw anything other than love and respect in my biological family, so when I married Jep, I expected to have great relationships with Phil and Miss Kay, and that's exactly what has happened.

I don't think anyone could ask for better in-laws than Phil and Miss Kay; they are everything I could have dreamed of, and I feel so blessed to have them. When Jep and I were first dating, I was going through a lot in my life, and they showed me love and forgiveness. Kay has so much love in her heart, and Phil is one of the wisest men I know.

I love the relationship Miss Kay and Phil have with each other. She respects and adores him. When Phil looks at Miss Kay or speaks to her, you can see in his eyes and hear in his voice that he thinks she is the best wife in the entire world. What I have observed since becoming part of the Robertson family is that Miss Kay has always taken care of Phil, and he has loved and cherished her. Even after many years together, they still laugh, they still love, and they still hug and kiss each other (even in front of the family and other people). Miss Kay still crawls into Phil's lap while he sits in his big recliner, and

> **When Phil looks at Miss Kay or speaks to her, you can see in his eyes and hear in his voice that he thinks she is the best wife in the entire world. —*Jessica***

when he walks close to her, he tickles her or gives her a pinch on the rear end.

Miss Kay and Phil have an amazing love for God and for people. They believe not only in giving second chances but also in giving third and fourth chances. When they need a little extra work done on their property, they often hire people who need help and try to help them as best they can. They spend hours and hours, several nights a week, counseling people and sharing their wisdom with them. If Jep and I can do even half of the good things Phil and Miss Kay have done, we will consider ourselves to have truly succeeded and made a difference in the world.

Missy: A TEAM OF SERVANTS

Phil and Miss Kay are definitely not typical in-laws. So many good qualities set Phil and Miss Kay apart from other people, but I think their best quality as a couple is their teamwork in serving others. They host many people in their home; they have always done this. Many of these people need wisdom, advice, salvation, or simply the knowledge that someone really cares about them.

Miss Kay used to cook all the meals and Phil used to do all the preaching and counseling. Over the years, they have realized that both of them have both of those strengths. Now Miss Kay and Phil both do the cooking, and they both sit down after the meal to talk with people, whether they are counseling a couple in a marriage crisis or sharing the message of Jesus with someone. They have grown together over the years and have recognized and embraced each other's strengths. This makes for a strong and godly marriage.

Korie: THEY JUST KEEP ON LOVING

Anyone who knows Miss Kay and Phil would have to say they are some of the most hospitable people anyone could ever find, anywhere. When I first met them, they did not have much money, but their home was always open. They lived in the same house they currently live in, but it was about half the size it is now. The kitchen was incredibly small, with no dishwasher, but that did not stop them from having guests regularly. They cooked huge, delicious meals out of that tiny kitchen, and everyone just gathered around standing or sitting on every available surface to enjoy the meal and laugh and talk together. They understood the true value of good conversation, good friends, good food, and family togetherness. Those things mattered more to them than anything else.

It's important to understand that the warm, fun, loving environment Miss Kay and Phil have created in their home did not happen automatically. In fact, it was years in the making. Miss Kay forgave Phil when a lot of people thought she had good reason not to, and she loved him when he was unlovable. The same dynamic happened to him that often happens when we truly understand that God forgives us and loves us when we are unlovable: it makes us want to do better and to be better. Miss Kay offered this to Phil, and he has done the same for her.

I'm sure there were times after Phil came to Christ that he still messed up, when he still sinned and fell short. Miss Kay had to forgive him, not just that one moment when he showed up outside her workplace begging her forgiveness, but many, many times after that. Forgiveness has to be offered over and over again in any marriage, and that was certainly true for Miss Kay and Phil. As in any husband-wife relationship, each person sometimes has to be the one who needs forgiving and sometimes has to be the one who does the forgiving.

Miss Kay showed God's love to Phil through her love and forgiveness, and he "got" it. Phil truly changed his life, and not just a little bit. He's not a lukewarm Christian by any means. He turned his life around totally and completely, and he now uses the gifts and talents God gave him for God's purposes rather than for his own selfish desires.

Now, with their most difficult years far behind them, Phil and Miss Kay show love continuously. They are playful with each other and laugh together all the time. They have weathered a lot of storms in their life together and are being rewarded for their faithfulness with a great marriage. It's so exciting for us to watch this couple who have been together for nearly fifty years continue to grow in their love for each other.

At any point either one of them could have given up. Had they done that, the rest of us would not be here today. People would not be watching our family on television, and lots of lives would have never been touched—not by us, at least. I know God is raising up others to do His work and touch many people, but I am proud that for this moment, for this time, He is using our family, and we will not take that for granted. We are grateful for the difficult choices Phil and Miss Kay made so we could all enjoy the close family and the good lives we have now.

Lisa: SO IN LOVE

Miss Kay and Phil know the pain I caused their son (more about that later), and they still chose to support us as a couple and chose to love and care for me. They have helped Alan and me in every way they possibly could through the years, whether that involved baby-sitting (Kay was the babysitter; Phil was the one who got credit for it on *Duck Dynasty*), financial support, or sharing their wisdom with us. Alan played an important role in the Duck Commander business during its early years, and they give him a lot of credit for that. This makes me proud for him and proud of him.

Miss Kay has always done a lot around the house for Phil. She has such a giving heart and is a natural caretaker, so she keeps an eye out for anything he needs or wants, and she accommodates him whenever possible. She is not one to grumble or complain about anything. She is a model of commitment, as everyone knows. She likes to bless other people, starting with Phil.

> **Miss Kay and Phil know the pain I caused their son, and they still chose to support us as a couple and chose to love and care for me.**
> *—Lisa*

Miss Kay is also respectful by nature. The respect with which she treats Phil made a deep impression on me when I first got to know them and continues to impress me today. One simple way

Miss Kay demonstrates respect for Phil is to keep in touch with him if she changes her plans throughout the day. She respects the fact that he needs to know where she is in case he should need to reach her for some really important reason (like asking her to stop at the store to pick up snuff). Especially if her schedule changes or if she is running late, she gives him a quick call and keeps him up-to-date on where she is. That's the kind of communication that keeps a relationship running smoothly. On top of all the good things Miss Kay does for Phil, she is totally, completely head over heels in love with him, as he is with her!

I know that Christ lives in Miss Kay and Phil, and they pattern their lives after His teachings. They truly practice what they preach. Together, they impact a lot of people in the most positive ways. Phil has a straightforward, up-front personality, while Miss Kay is understanding and comforting. That's a great combination. When the two of them counsel people who need help or guidance, especially couples who are struggling in their marriages, the people they help leave believing they can conquer the world together.

11

PASSING IT ON

A Message from the Daughters-in-Law

Miss Kay and Phil are terrific grandparents to our children. We are always glad when the children—whether they are very young or whether they are young adults—can be with them because they always learn something valuable and because they come away knowing they are loved in very special ways. Miss Kay and Phil have established a powerful legacy of love and faith from which all of our children can benefit. They have so many good qualities to pass on to their grandchildren, and we look forward to seeing how these qualities manifest in their lives in the future.

Lisa: GREAT RELATIONSHIPS

My children are grown, but my daughters have a great relationship with Miss Kay and Phil. In fact, Miss Kay is both of my girls' best friend. Both Anna and Alex have kind, loving, gentle hearts, and I know they learned these qualities from Miss Kay. I was not always the mother I needed to be for my children, but Miss Kay took up the slack, and they are awesome women today because of her.

Both girls have spent a lot of time with Miss Kay and Phil over the years. Anna started working for Miss Kay as a teenager, and although she now works full-time at Duck Commander, she also does special projects for Miss Kay and travels with her as much as possible. When asked about her relationship with Kay, Anna says, "I have been close to Mamaw Kay all my life, but even more so since I started working for her when I was fourteen or fifteen. Some people have grandmas they cannot open up to, but I can talk about *every-thing* with Mamaw Kay. I always turn to her when I need someone to talk to, and she gives really good advice. She knows about so many things because she has been there; she has lived it. And I can trust her. If I need to talk to her about something I do not want her to share, she will *not* tell it.

"Plus, Mamaw Kay is great when it comes to fashion. She knows what's in style and stays up on trends, and I like that about her. But most of all, I have noticed in my life that some grandparents are quick to say 'I love you,' but they do not always do much to show it. With Mamaw Kay, I have always felt loved, and I know I always will. Every time we get together, when it's time to go, we give each other a big hug and say, 'I love you!' I know Mamaw Kay really means those words when she says them to me, and I really mean them when I say them to her."

Phil has always had a special place for my girls in his heart, but when they were young, he did not always know how to show it. As the years have mellowed him, he now has a great, loving relation-ship with my granddaughters. They adore Papaw Phil. My daughters are old enough to understand and appreciate all of Phil and Miss Kay's good qualities. I believe they will inherit all of those attitudes and characteristics (they already demonstrate a lot of them), and I pray they will pass them down to their own children.

Missy: A Lot to Learn

We all have so much to learn from Miss Kay and Phil. My prayer and hope is that my children have learned the valuable life lessons they have to share. I hope my children have learned from Phil and Miss Kay to look at everyone they meet with a nonjudgmental heart. I hope they have learned and will continue to learn that judgment belongs to God and we are here only to guide people to Him. I hope they have learned to laugh at the little things and the big things and to know that God has given them this life as a gift.

I hope my kids have learned a strong work ethic by watching their papaw Phil work on the land and in the yard cleaning fish, deer, and ducks. I hope they learn to be generous in feeding fam-ily, friends, and even strangers a good, home-cooked meal and that having an open-door policy is much more fulfilling than a closed, locked door with a security system. Most of all, I hope they have watched their grandparents stay real in an unreal world, learned that they can turn to God for all of their problems,

> I hope my children have learned from Phil and Miss Kay to look at everyone they meet with a nonjudgmental heart. —*Missy*

and come to understand that they can love people enough to share that same God with everyone they meet.

Korie: STRENGTH, LOVE, AND COMPASSION

The three traits I have tried to instill in my children since they were born are strength, love, and compassion. Both Phil and Miss Kay exemplify these traits, even though they express them in different ways. I hope my children will continue to develop strength based on a deep knowledge of *whose* they are (God's) and understand that His power moves mountains. I pray they will always love others but love God above all else. I also hope and pray they will consistently demonstrate compassion by treating others with kindness and humility. They certainly see these qualities in their grandparents. I can already see these same traits unfolding in my children, and I look forward to seeing these good characteristics mature in them over the years to come.

Jessica: LEAVING A LEGACY

Phil and Miss Kay will definitely leave a legacy of love for God, love for each other, and love for people in general. They both truly love and care for others, regardless of a person's skin color or economic status, and will help anyone in any way they can. They are not very technological; they value quality time with people and good conversations over text messages and e-mail. They want everyone with whom they come in contact to know God. Both of them are dedicated to family and to the togetherness that comes from the family table, and I hope these things will continue in my children and throughout the generations of Robertsons to come.

I hope my children will always love to read and love to cook, as Miss Kay does. I pray they will inherit the way Miss Kay cheers for the underdog, lifts the brokenhearted, and gives to anyone in need. I hope they will also notice and learn from the fact that she loves and respects Phil and is a loyal, committed wife and friend to him.

I feel that my children have a rare opportunity to glean from Phil some things that have been lost in modern society. In many ways, he is "old school." He still works his land and takes care of it, which is important for them to see. He is hardworking, industrious, and resourceful. He could not care less about the things of this world; he is totally nonmaterialistic but is a man who hungers and thirsts to know God. Sometimes I am amazed to see him studying his Bible in his recliner because he already knows it so well. But he continues to study diligently. His desire to walk in truth is deep, and his faithfulness to God is remarkable. I hope my children absorb these things from Phil and incorporate them into their lives to the greatest possible degree.

I also want our children, boy and girls, to have a love for the outdoors like Phil and Miss Kay have. Miss Kay loves nature and has a special affection for all kinds of animals. Phil loves having the ability to provide for his family through growing vegetables, fishing, frogging, and hunting deer and ducks. All of that knowledge from both of them has been passed to us, and it is so important that the generations who come after us not lose the ability to live off the land. Jep and I are actively teaching our children survival skills, in addition to the skills they observe and learn from Phil and Miss Kay.

I don't mean to imply that we never buy meat or vegetables at the grocery store; we simply have the skills and ability to provide for our family from what God has created, and we have a love and appreciation for the outdoors, which Jep and I both got from our families.

I am aware that some people don't like "meat eaters" because they think we are killing animals for the sake of killing, but that is not true. We are providing food for our family. One of my favorite meats to eat is deer. You can't get a leaner, more healthy meat. I like certain parts of the deer better than others, but we do not waste anything. We often take deer meat and ducks to local neighborhoods in which people may not have the money to buy meat, and we just give it to them. We also share meat with widows in our church. The looks on their faces when we do this are priceless.

This combination of living off the land, being resourceful, not wasting anything, and sharing with others comes from Phil and Miss Kay. It's the kind of thing they do, it's what Jep and I do, and it's what we are teaching our children to do.

Part Three

HAPPILY EVER AFTER CAN TAKE A WHILE

We also rejoice in our sufferings, because we know that suffering produces perseverance; perseverance, character; and character, hope.

ROMANS 5:3–4

12

INTRODUCTION

Miss Kay

I just love to read. I especially love to read to my grandchildren. In fact, at my house, I set up a little library for them. They can go in there, look through the books, choose some to read, and then sign their names on a piece of paper to "check out" the books like I used to do before so many libraries got computers. Like any good librarian, I want to make sure I get my books back so other children can enjoy them!

When I was a child, my favorite stories were ones that ended with the words "and they lived happily ever after." My grandchildren like that kind of ending too. But what I know, and what they have not yet learned, is that "happily ever after" sometimes takes a while.

I learned the hard way how long a happy ending can take and how difficult it can be. So

> **I learned the hard way how long a happy ending can take and how difficult it can be.**
>
> —*Miss Kay*

did my daughter-in-law Lisa. Both of us want to share our stories with you. We do not necessarily enjoy talking about the heartache and struggles we have been through, but we want to talk about them because we want you to have hope for any disappointing or devastating situation in your life and to know that God is always in the business of healing and restoration, no matter how bad the circumstances might be.

13

I FOUND OUT WHAT IT MEANS TO FIGHT

Miss Kay

My grandmother once told me, "You'll have to fight for your marriage." When she said those words, I did not understand them. I had no idea what she meant. I never really saw her fight for her marriage because she had a good relationship with my grandfather. I would not say they were lovey-dovey all the time, but they treated each other with respect and there was peace in their home.

In the early years of my marriage to Phil, I did everything I could think of to be a good wife and a good mother to Alan. I had all kinds of dreams about a happy marriage and a loving family, and I honestly believed if I worked hard enough, those dreams would come true. They didn't, no matter how hard I tried—at least not for a long, long time.

I was pregnant with Alan when Phil and I moved to Ruston, Louisiana, for him to attend college and play football at Louisiana

Tech. Phil was *really* good! In fact, when he left the team a couple of years later, his replacement was a guy who was also really good, but not as good as Phil. That second-string quarterback was named Terry Bradshaw, and he went on to become a very famous football player.

BAD COMBINATIONS

The football team and everything that went along with being a player did not provide a good environment for Phil. After spring training of his first year, he had to spend some time living in a dorm with his teammates—a bunch of single guys out from under their parents' watchful eyes for the first time. They enjoyed drinking and partying, and because Phil was the star quarterback, they always wanted him to join them. He was young, like the other guys on the football team, and some of them told him he was really missing something because he had never had his "wild time." I guess he believed them, because he got wild pretty fast and started drinking with his buddies. When that happened, I tried to be with him without getting involved in all the things he was doing. I went to some parties, but when the drinking started, all I could think about was my mother and what alcohol had done to her. Besides, I had enough sense to know that drinking and being pregnant did not go together. So Phil started sowing his wild oats, while I stayed sober and scared of what was happening to him.

During this time, Phil and I did not go to church. He didn't want to. He did not have his own faith at that point, and neither did I.

Both of us grew up attending church, but once we were out on our own we were free to choose whether we would continue or not. Part of me wanted to go, but I believed Phil was the head of our household and I needed to do what he wanted, which was to stay home on Sunday mornings. Another part of me did not want to go because I was young and pregnant and unmarried, and I felt embarrassed. I kept thinking we would go to church later, in a year or two when we got married and things settled down. I had no idea how bad our lives would get before we finally did.

After Alan was born, I had my hands full. I was very young, and of course I had never had a baby before. I did not have much help or support, but I was determined to be a good mother and that took a lot of my time and energy. I could not stay out late at night partying with Phil and I certainly was not going to get drunk.

One night, I had a major reality check. Phil and I were at a party and had taken Alan. One of Phil's good friends from home was also in school at Tech. His wife was a good friend of mine and they lived close to us. We were all together at a party one weekend and my friend suggested I check on Alan. He was throwing up. I wrapped him in a blanket, found Phil, and said, "We have to go home. The baby's sick." Phil would not leave the party, so I took Alan home alone. There's no telling when Phil showed up. That night was the end of my party time. From then on, Phil partied and drank, but I did not go with him. I remember being so torn inside because I really wanted to be with Phil. At the same time, when I thought about those parties and everything that went on during them, all I could say to myself was, "I can't do this. I just can't do it." I didn't; I quit all of that, but Phil kept on.

THINGS WILL GET BETTER

I truly believed Phil would leave his wild ways behind once he finished college, got away from his football buddies, and started working. Even though he didn't make a priority of his studies and eventually left the football team so he could spend more time hunting and fishing, Phil graduated with both a bachelor's and a master's degree. He was well prepared to be a teacher and a coach. I was so excited about the next stage of our lives, convinced things would be better and that the happy home life I always dreamed of would finally come true.

Phil got a job soon after graduation. A man named Al Bolen recruited him as a teacher in Junction City, Arkansas. I was so happy when I realized the school was going to provide us with a little house and I could work as the school secretary. Finally, just as I had hoped, everything was shaping up just as I wanted it to. We even lived across the street from a sweet elderly couple, an old preacher and his wife, who was blind. They took an interest in Alan as soon as they met him. They loved him, and he loved them. They took him to church every Sunday, starting when he was five years old. The preacher and Alan really had an amazing relationship, and I was so thankful for that.

After Jase was born, the preacher and his wife took him to church, too, and sometimes I went with them. Phil still was not interested in church at that point, except when his parents, Granny and Pa, came to visit. When his parents were with us, we all went to church, but Phil was miserable. Phil has never been a person to pretend. Everything is black or white, good or bad, with him. If he likes something, he lets it be known. If he doesn't like something, he does not keep it to himself. He did not like church, and everyone knew it.

Maybe one reason he did not like church was that he had not left behind his drinking and partying when we moved from Ruston. Al Bolen turned out to be a big fisherman and duck hunter, just like Phil, but he also had a drinking problem, which was the last thing Phil needed to be around. Instead of finally being able to live my dream in Arkansas, I was right back in the same old nightmare.

MOVING ON

By the time Willie was born, people in the community were aware of Phil's behavior. He did not drink every day; he could go days or even weeks without taking a sip. He was a party guy. When he got around other people and started drinking, he did not stop until he was good and drunk. In a small town, word travels fast when people do things like that, especially when those people are schoolteachers. The school administration and students' parents finally began to lose their patience with Phil, and he knew he would soon be fired. He decided to get another job and move our family out of town before that happened. With my Pollyanna attitude and my firm belief that everything would get better if I could just be the perfect wife and mother, I hoped a new start would be exactly what we needed. It wasn't.

Phil's personal situation, our marriage, and our family life got worse. Phil decided to leave teaching and coaching, and, as he put it, "make some money." Without even mentioning to me what he wanted to do, he leased a bar in a rural area of Arkansas! We lived in a trailer next door to it. All I could think was, *Seriously? You are going to run a bar in the middle of nowhere? What am I supposed to do, take my kids to a bar every night?* I knew I would have to help Phil in this new business, but I did not know anything about running a bar. I didn't even drink!

By this time, I had thought a lot about our marriage and family. It was not turning out the way I dreamed it would, not even close. I was disappointed, of course, but more than that, I was at a total loss about what to do. I knew that if I talked to my sister, she would tell me to leave Phil. One of Phil's brothers had already said I needed to leave. But I couldn't get my grandmother's advice out of my head: "You're going to have to fight for your marriage." I was finding out what those words meant, and the fight was a whole lot worse than I ever thought it could be.

Although some people thought I had a good reason to leave Phil when we got ready to move out of town so he could run the bar, I decided to go with him. I knew he could end up in big, big trouble— and I thought I could protect him. If not, at least I could keep an eye on him and at least our three little boys would have both parents in the home with them.

Once Phil started operating the bar, I went to work as a barmaid. It was the only way I knew to keep up with what he was doing. The local people who visited the bar knew immediately that I did not belong there. They kept telling me I needed to be in church, not waiting tables in a bar. I got the feeling they would have fought to the death for me. They thought I was a "nice lady"; they really respected me and refused to let anybody say anything bad about me. They did not understand why I worked in the bar when it seemed so out of character for me, but they also did not understand it was about much more than serving drinks for tips every night: I was fighting with all my might to save my marriage.

During this time, I found an elderly lady who babysat the boys while Phil and I worked, so thankfully they were not exposed to many of the things I saw and experienced. So many unsafe things happened, and I spent a lot of time frightened and anxious about what we should do. There were times when Phil started drinking and simply disappeared for a few days, leaving me alone with three boys and a run-down bar. When that happened, an elderly man who lived in the area ran the bar, while I kept serving drinks and wondering when Phil would come home.

OUR DARKEST DAYS

Phil became cold and harsh during those days. He was mean and threatening to me, and I was terrified of what would happen to my boys and me. Even though I had not been in church because I was so embarrassed about everything that was happening and about Phil's behavior, I did make sure the boys got there every Sunday and I never forgot my Christian upbringing. One day, I began to pray with all my heart, "God, just get us out of here."

Somehow, we made it through the first year of Phil's lease on the bar, even though it was a terrible time. Three or four months later, the landlords showed up one day and cussed out Phil, saying they did not like the way he was running the place and were raising his rent. They were rough people, and I think what they *really* didn't like was that Phil had turned the place into a profitable business and was making good money off it.

Those people were not smart. They had no idea that trying to push Phil Robertson around and cuss him out would lead to disaster. He got so angry with them that he beat them up—both of them. By the time I got to the bar to try to figure out what was happening, all I saw were people being loaded into an ambulance.

During all the confusion, Phil did the only thing he knew to do: run away. He told me quickly that he was leaving and he would be gone for a while, just before he slipped out a back door. I knew he would be in trouble with the law and the only way to avoid that would be for him to hide out. He told me to handle the situation the best I could and then leave. I faced five police cars that night and enough questions to make my head spin. They wanted Phil, and I could honestly tell them I had no idea where they might find him.

> So there I was: no source of income, husband on the run, three little boys, in the middle of Arkansas. Phil had made a huge mess of our lives. —*Miss Kay*

So there I was: no source of income, husband on the run, three little boys, in the middle of Arkansas. Phil had made a huge mess of our lives and had left me to clean it up. I felt completely helpless and hopeless.

When the couple who owned the bar got out of the hospital, they put up a barricade around my trailer. The boys and I were trapped! I couldn't move the trailer and I couldn't leave. One day they said they wanted to meet with me, and I had no choice but to talk to them. They offered to drop the charges against Phil if I would pay them a certain amount of money. It was extortion, but I paid them because it was the only way I knew to clear Phil's name and get the boys and myself away from them. I gave them almost all the money we had except a little bit that was in a lockbox, and they gave me the trailer. I also had some things stored in another building on their property—some keepsakes and things that held special memories for me—and a washer and dryer. They would not let me get near any of those things, so I had to leave them all behind.

FROM BAD TO WORSE

I hired a moving company to move the trailer from Arkansas to Bayou D'Arbonne Lake, near Farmerville, Louisiana. I had told Phil in a phone call where he could find us, and he soon came out of the swamp and joined us. He was so relieved when I told him he would not be arrested over the incident with the bar owners. While he was on the run, he had found a job in an offshore oil field, but we still needed money, so I went to work at a local chicken place and made just enough to pay our electric bill.

Phil was drinking worse than ever by that time, and I began to get seriously depressed. Not only were my hopes and dreams shattered, I couldn't even figure out how to make anything in our lives work. Everything was falling apart.

I soon got a new job as an insurance clerk in Monroe, Louisiana, a little less than thirty miles from our new home on the lake. The company that hired me was Howard Brothers Discount Stores, the family business of my daughter-in-law Korie, though she was only a few years old at the time and I had no idea who she was. It's a good thing I had a decent job, because not long after I got it, Phil was hurt offshore and had to stay home. I was afraid to leave the boys with him, not knowing what he might do if he drank too much, so I put them in day care.

As the situation continued, I grew more and more depressed. I worked with two Christian men at Howard Brothers, and every day, one of them would give me a Bible verse, just to try to encourage me. Those verses gave me the strength I needed to get through this terrible time in my life.

One rainy night, I had car trouble and was late picking up the boys from day care. When we finally got home, Phil accused me of having an affair! It was ridiculous. When was I going to find time to have an affair—between working full-time and changing diapers? I had always told him I would never cheat, and I would not have. I never believed in being unfaithful; it's just not in my character.

That cheating accusation was the last straw for me. I hit rock bottom. I have never felt as totally hopeless as I did that night. I simply could not see any way out of a terrible situation for the boys and me. I finally accepted the fact that I could not fix our lives and had no one to help. So I did what a lot of women do when they need to be alone: I went into the bathroom and locked the door. I cried and cried, and finally realized I just wanted to go to sleep for a long time. I did not consciously want to kill myself; I just wanted to take enough Tylenol (because that's all we had) to have a nice, long rest. And I wanted to scare the daylights out of Phil. I wanted to punish him for everything he had put me through. I told myself I didn't care if I slept forever, but deep down I don't think I really wanted to die.

In the midst of that low place, the darkest place I have ever been emotionally, with thoughts of sleep and rest filling my mind, through my sobs I heard the scurry of little feet headed toward the bathroom door. I could tell all three boys, in their house shoes, were coming to talk to me. Alan spoke first: "Mom, don't cry. Don't cry anymore. God will take care of us." I was silent for a moment. Then I heard Jase ask, "Did she quit crying?" And I could hear Willie doing something he did often, making smacking noises while sucking on two of his fingers.

In an instant, it was like a lightbulb came on for me. "What am I doing?" I asked myself. "I have three little boys. I can't leave them with a drunk."

I spoke to my sons through the door: "I'm okay. I love y'all. I'll be out in a minute."

I then got on my knees and prayed. "God, help me. Just help me. I don't want to leave these kids. I don't know what to do or where to find You. Just lead me to somebody who can help me."

PEACE, HOPE, AND LOVE

The next day, I saw a television commercial for some kind of religious TV show. The ad said something like, "Do you want peace, hope, and a reason for living? Do you want someone to love you and never let you go?" I turned up the volume just as the announcer said, "Then call this number."

So I called that number and told the woman who answered, "I want to speak with that man who is on TV talking about peace, hope, and love. It's an emergency. I need to talk to him right away."

The man's name was Bill Smith. When I saw him, I knew exactly who he was. Phil's sister was a member of his church, and months earlier she had brought him to the bar hoping he could talk some sense into Phil, but Phil would not listen to him. I didn't care whether Phil wanted to hear what Bill Smith had to say or not. I did.

When I got to his church, White's Ferry Road Church, and met with him, the first question he asked me was if I thought I would go to heaven when I died.

"Of course I'd go to heaven. You have no idea what I have been through and what I have put up with from my husband." Then I told him how hard I had fought for my marriage and how faithful I had been, even though Phil had done terrible things.

The preacher asked me if I thought I had earned my way to heaven. I certainly did!

He then asked me if I had any peace or hope in my life. That was my problem. My peace and hope had run out years earlier. I now see what a disconnect was going on in my mind. I thought I had earned my way to God, but I wasn't at peace and I had lost all hope.

He then shared the gospel with me, and I realized two things. First, I realized I never really had my own faith. For many years, I'd lived off my grandmother's faith, but faith was not deeply personal for me. Second, I saw that I really was a good person, but I was a good person without Jesus Christ, and I desperately needed Him. That very day, before I left the church, I confessed to Jesus, made Him Lord of my life, and was baptized. Needless to say, I felt so much better! I had peace in my heart, and best of all, I had hope again.

Everyone in the church that day was so happy for me. The janitor, the housekeeper, and the church secretary all gave me big hugs. "You're part of our family now! We'll be there for you, and you can be there for us," they said.

That's nice, I thought, *but my husband is a drunk.*

AT LEAST ONE OF US CHANGED

Preacher Smith was a very wise man. He knew that no matter what had happened for me that day, nothing at all had happened for Phil. He gave me a clear warning before I went home, telling me that even though I had become a Christian and I would never be alone and God would never leave me, that didn't mean Phil would act any better. He would still be the same person I had struggled with for years. He would still get drunk, be mean, and do the same things he had always done.

I continued to stay with Phil because I knew God would help me. I prayed and prayed for him; the boys did too. I would invite the preacher over to talk to Phil and Phil would slip out the back door as the preacher came in the front, and he sometimes stayed gone for days. But I was still determined to fight for my marriage. Then one night I was late coming home from work and Phil again accused me of running around on him. He yelled at me, saying he was sick of me. He said I was bad to live with before, but now I was a holy roller and a goody-two-shoes. According to Phil at the time, I thought I was "the judge of the world." I did not think that at all. I was just trying to stay sane and keep my boys safe.

At that point, Phil said angrily, "You are messing up my life. I can't live with you. I want you and your kids to get out."

"I have fought for this marriage," I replied, "and you are kicking me out?"

Yes he was. He wanted me gone from his life. When I tell this story, I make a point to emphasize the fact that *I did not leave*. I got thrown out, and I was heartbroken.

> **Phil said angrily, "You are messing up my life. I can't live with you. I want you and your kids to get out."**
> —*Miss Kay*

The boys and I went to a relative's house, and I was hoping we could stay there for a while. But even though this man was a close relative on Phil's side of the family, he would only allow us in his home for one night. He was just as afraid of Phil as I was, maybe more so. He was terrified of what Phil might do to him and his family if Phil knew we were staying with them.

MY CHURCH BECOMES MY FAMILY

The only people I knew to turn to was my church family. I knew the people at White's Ferry Road would help me. Someone there helped me arrange an income-based apartment. When I took a relative to the place I had been living with Phil so we could get the things the boys and I needed, she saw how hurt I was, and she was angry with Phil for the way he had treated the boys and me. She suggested we destroy everything that belonged to him. I had one answer for that:

"I don't retaliate." As much as Phil had hurt me, hurting him in return went against my nature and, by then, against my Christian beliefs.

In our little apartment, the boys and I had a very small television. We'd had a larger one when we lived with Phil, but he'd kept it and the boys really missed it. I told them I didn't care what kind of TV we had; we needed to be focused on studying the Bible. So that's what we did; we studied the Bible and we all got on our knees and prayed for Phil, every day.

Even though Phil had treated me badly, there was a hole in my heart after he kicked out the boys and me. I so desperately wanted God to change him. I prayed, the boys prayed, and I got everybody I knew to pray with us. My friends at work prayed for our family; I took Bible classes at church and asked everyone in every class to pray for my husband. I even remember standing in line at Walmart one day and asking the woman behind me, "Do you pray?" When she said yes, I told her about Phil. I knew only God could change things for us and that the way to get to Him was through prayer.

About three months later, I went to lunch one day with a friend from work. When we returned to the Howard Brothers offices, I saw Phil's old truck in the parking lot. My friend asked me if I wanted her to call the police, and I said, "No, I'll go talk to him. Just watch me through the window. If anything happens, then call them." As I walked toward the truck and saw Phil bent over the steering wheel, I assumed he was drunk. He was not; he was crying. I opened the door of the truck and for the first time in my life saw huge tears flowing down his face. I'll never forget what he said: "I can't sleep. I can't eat. I want my family back, and I am never going to drink again."

My first thought was, *This is the man I want. This one, right here.* But I had enough sense not to say that right away.

"Phil, you can't do it by yourself," I told him. "You need help. You really need help."

"Are you talking about God?" he asked.

"Yep, that's it," I answered.

"I don't know how to find Him," said Phil.

"Well, I do," I responded. "You be back in this parking lot at five o'clock and follow me home. I'll have someone there to talk to you."

Phil agreed. Back in my office, I called Bill Smith, told him what happened, and asked him to come to my apartment at five fifteen that evening to talk to Phil. He said he would have to check his calendar.

"*Check your calendar?*" I said, almost in disbelief. "What on earth could be more important than this lost soul?"

He must have realized I was right, because he immediately said, "I'll be there."

THE TURNAROUND BEGINS

When Phil walked into our apartment that night, the boys were so happy. The first thing they wanted to know was whether he'd brought back the big TV. All Phil could say was, "I didn't know I was supposed to do that." He looked around the sparse room where we had been living and said, "You should have gotten more stuff." It never was about stuff to me. The last thing we needed during that time was more stuff.

Bill Smith and his wife, Margaret, arrived right at five fifteen. Phil looked at him and immediately said, "I don't trust people."

Smith held up his copy of the Bible and asked, "Do you trust this?"

"Yes," said Phil. "And I am going to check out everything you say."

The preacher said to me, "Get a pencil so Phil can write everything down."

Margaret and I took the boys into a little back room and we prayed and prayed while Phil talked with the preacher.

When their visit was over, Phil said, "I'm not going to do any of this until I check it out."

Bill Smith came back and helped Phil study the Bible the next night and the night after that. I let Phil stay in the apartment with us, and he was so humble. He loved the boys—and that made all of us happy. The change in him was like night and day. The fourth night, I believe, I got home from work one evening, expecting to find Bill Smith and Phil studying the Bible, but I didn't see them anywhere. Our apartment was so small I didn't have to look very far. I can't remember now whether they did not leave a note or whether I just didn't see it, but I had no idea where they were, so I went to the church to look for them. When I got there, Phil was getting baptized!

That was just like Phil—to make up his mind to do something and then not even tell me or wait for me to get there after I had prayed so long and hard for that moment. It was okay, though. As long as he made Jesus Christ his Lord and Savior, I was happy.

Things did not change for us overnight, but they did change over time. Phil stopped drinking very quickly, and once he started

studying the Bible, he never stopped. At times, as God was changing him, he had to suffer the consequences of some of the things
he had done, but he has thoroughly and completely changed from
the man he used to be. After a lot of hurt and disappointment, and
a lot of prayer, God really did change him. He is now the kindest,
most loving man I have ever known, and he is fearless about sharing his faith because he knows how much God changed his life. I can
honestly say, after those terrible times in our early years, Phil truly
became the man of my dreams.

14

HAVE HOPE

Lisa

As I mentioned earlier, I fell for Alan when I was in the sixth grade. When we finally got married, after some drama in both of our lives individually and in our relationship, I was thrilled! In our early days of marriage, I thought Alan walked on water. He was wonderful! My thinking he was too wonderful got our marriage off to a bad start, but I did not know that for several years. I did not realize I not only loved Alan, I actually worshipped him. He was more important to me than God was, and I had a greater love for him than I did for God. Having a terrific husband is a blessing, but when a wife gives her husband the worship God deserves, trouble is on its way.

Within the first five years of our marriage, we had two beautiful daughters. I wish I could say we lived happily ever after, and ultimately we did. But we went through a painful process to get there, a process that began when I was just a little girl.

I Should Have Been Safe

I was the youngest of three children in my family. My brother was twelve years older than I, and my sister was seven years older. Because I was so much younger than my siblings and my mom worked outside the home, I spent most of my time at my grandmother's house. Until I started school, I was at her house five days a week. After I started school, I stayed with her every day during the summertime.

One of my favorite things about being at my grandmother's house was that she served eggs, bacon, biscuits, and sweet tea for breakfast. I do have some pleasant memories of being there, as a lot of people do, but I have a lot that are not so pleasant because something tragic happened to me at my grandmother's house, something that damaged me deeply and haunted my life for years.

One of the things Miss Kay and I have in common is that both of us understand firsthand how dangerous alcohol can be to a family. Miss Kay dealt with her mother's alcohol use and later, to a much greater degree, with Phil's problem. A number of people in my family abused alcohol, and both of my siblings eventually died young because of it.

As a little girl, I had an extended family member who had major drug and alcohol problems. Unfortunately, that person lived with my grandparents, so I had to see him often. Because I spent so much time at my grandparents' house, I was easy prey for him. My earliest memory of being molested was at the age of seven when he started to do things to me, things that made me feel bad and dirty. I don't

One of my favorite outfits as a child—my jeans, boots, and cowgirl hat.

Me with my older sister, Ann, and our father.

My grandfather with his plow, behind Tony and me.

Nannie's mother, my great-grandmother.

Miss Kay

Even as a little girl, I was obviously comfortable and happy at the table!

My papaw Carroway, my dad's father.

When Phil and I met, he was a football player and I was a cheerleader. Here I am in my uniform.

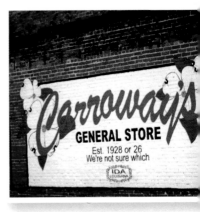

This sign commemorates my daddy's store in Ida, Louisiana.

A picture from my beauty pageant days.

Phil, about the time I met him. Is it any wonder I fell for him?

No matter what I was going through, I always took good care of my boys. Here I am with Alan *(right)* and Jase *(left)*.

Phil and me with Alan *(left)* and Jase *(right)*, in our early days.

I love being a grandmother. Here are my two oldest grandchildren, Anna *(left)* and Alex *(right)*, with me at the beach.

The Duck Commander and me. We've been through a lot!

Here I am, accessorized with hat and necklace!

Willie and me at our college club banquet. One of the few pics of Willie in a tie.

This was at our engagement party. Willie and I were so excited to be starting our life together.

We were young, but we were happy—and we still are! Willie and me on our wedding day, January 11, 1992.

Willie and me, with the city of
Florence, Italy, in the background,
during our college trip to Europe.
Great memories!

Look at that cutie! Willie and me
at the Atlanta Olympics, 1996.

Two people for whom I'm
extremely grateful: my parents,
Johnny and Chrys Howard.
Looking good!

Four generations!
Mamaw Shack, Mom,
me, and John Luke.

Our first little vacation afte
Bella was born. We went to
Hot Springs, Arkansas. Our
hands and hearts were full!
From left: Will, John Luke,
me, Sadie, Willie, Bella.

Korie

Mamaw and Papaw Shack with John Luke and Sadie. Thankful for their love and example.

So thankful for a godly heritage. Sadie with Mamaw and Papaw Howard.

ki trip with my parents to teamboat, Colorado, in 2012. ront row: Bella. Middle row: adie, John Luke, Will. Back w: Two-Mama (my mom), wo-Papa (my dad), Willie, me.

Love our family! Front row: Bella. Back row: Will, Sadie, Willie, me, Rebecca, John Luke.

Me as a child. Obviously, it was school picture day!

"Go, Eagles!" Me in my cheerleading uniform during my freshman year at Ouachita Christian School.

Jase and me, before we had children, in our 1992 church pictorial directory. See? I told you he is really handsome underneath that beard!

Beardless Robertson boys with Miss Kay. *From left:* Willie, Alan, Miss Kay, Jase, Jep.

Missy

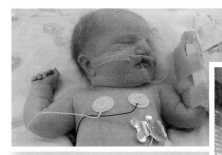

Mia as a newborn. She has overcome so much!

Mia, at approximately three weeks old, before her first surgery.

A beautiful room for our baby girl. This is the room Miss Kay and others surprised me with before Mia was born.

My family with my parents and Miss Kay. *From left:* Miss Kay, Jase, Cole, Mia, Reed, me, my mom, and my dad at the Ouachita Christian School Homecoming presentation in 2011.

My parents and me, in front of the Ouachita Christian School flag. They helped found the school with four other couples in 1974.

Missy

My aunt, Bonny, who is like my sister, and me at Sadie's Sweet Sixteen birthday party in 2013.

Miss Kay, a great mother-in-law and friend, and me one Mother's Day.

Remember the duck that Jase missed and I shot? Here it is, with Mia and me.

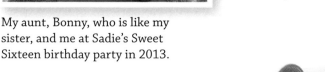

Family vacation. This group goes to the beach together every year. Standing next to Miss Kay is her sister, Ann.

Jessica

My sister, Stacy, and me one Christmas.

My wonderful new in-laws! Miss Kay, Phil, Jep, and me right after our wedding.

Jep with his brothers on our wedding day. *From left:* Jase, Alan, Jep, Willie.

Granny with Merritt, her namesake. Granny was so proud to have a great-grandchild named after her.

Lily as a little cowgirl.

Miss Kay and me in front of Christmas decorations.

My parents, Terry and Kathy Strickland, with Jep, me, and the kids.

Jep and me with the girls before River was born. *Front row from left:* Merritt, Priscilla, Lily.

The Robertson women beachside. *From left:* Lisa, Korie, Miss Kay, me, Missy.

Jessica

Our girls, in beautiful dresses, with River. *Back row:* Priscilla. *Front row:* Lily, River, Merritt.

Jep and me with our children at Miss Kay and Phil's vow renewal in 2013. *Back row:* Jep, me. *Front row:* Lily, Merritt, River (making a face!), Priscilla.

The kids share a loving moment. *Back row:* Lily, Merritt, Priscilla. *Front row:* River.

Lisa

A school photograph.

Happy couple! Alan and me at our wedding reception.

Anna as a newborn. She was born at twenty-nine weeks.

Two women who taught me so much. Granny and Miss Kay with Anna and Alex.

A powerful picture of God's restoration and healing power. Alan and me with our granddaughters, Carley *(left)* and Bailey *(right)*.

Lisa

Miss Kay is both of my girls' best friend. Here are *(from left)* Alex and Anna with their mamaw Kay.

Our family at Anna's wedding. *From left:* me, Alan, Anna, Jay, Alex.

Our daughter Anna with some of the special men in her life.

A special moment for Alex. Alan officiated her wedding ceremony, so Papaw Phil walked her down the aisle.

Lisa

Our daughter Alex and her husband, Vinny, at Alex's wedding, with the Robertson men and Miss Kay. *From left:* Si, Jase, Alan, Willie, Phil, Miss Kay, Jep, Alex, Vinny.

From left: me, my sister, Barbara, and my mom, Maudie.

They call me Mam. My granddaughters and me at pumpkin patch.

Alan and me with Phil and Miss Kay. I have such love and respect for my in-laws.

Still going strong. Alan and me at the beach.

remember how he threatened me (every abuser threatens) if I ever told anyone about it, but whatever he said worked. Chances are, he probably told me my dad would be upset with me if he found out. I adored my dad, and I would never have done anything to upset him. The abuser knew that.

One morning at my grandmother's house, I became very frightened and called my mother at work, begging her to come get me and take me home. I would not tell her why I wanted to leave, so she probably thought I had gotten into trouble with my grandparents. I don't remember what triggered my fear, but my mother did not come get me that day. I never told her or my dad about the abuse.

The abuser continued to abuse me whenever I visited my grandmother's house until I was about fourteen years old, when my grandfather died. During a big family gathering at my grandmother's house after the funeral, he got me alone. He was planning to continue his actions right after we'd buried my grandfather! But that time was different. I had had enough. I finally stood up for myself and told him that if he ever touched me again I would tell my dad and my dad would kill him. I am *positive* I was right about that.

> My earliest memory of being molested was at the age of seven when he started to do things to me, things that made me feel bad and dirty. —*Lisa*

After many years, I did tell my mother about the abuse because she babysat my grandchildren and I wanted to make sure they were protected. I also forgave the abuser eventually, but not for a long time—and not without first being personally devastated, not without deeply wounding the people I love most, and not without ultimately going through a powerful experience of having someone forgive me.

UNFORTUNATELY, IT'S NOT UNCOMMON

As I thought about writing this book, I wanted to share about the abuse for a couple of reasons. First, what happened to me happens to many, many people. It's tragic, but it's common. Second, I want all abuse survivors to know they have hope. They can have hope for complete healing, hope for great relationships, and hope for a wonderful life, free from the lingering effects of the trauma they have suffered. I say this with complete confidence because after a lot of help from special people and a lot of healing from God, it happened for me.

Sexual abuse is always physically damaging; it's also emotionally damaging, and most people recognize that. I would like to add that for me, it was mentally damaging. Let me explain. Being abused did something to the way I thought about myself and about men in general. It set in motion some unhealthy thought processes that took root

> To put it simply, I unconsciously began to believe my purpose in life was to please men.
> —*Lisa*

in my mind without my knowledge—and certainly without my agreement—and stayed in place for many years. To put it simply, I unconsciously began to believe my purpose in life was to please men. Therefore, because the abuse happened at such a young age, I never developed a healthy sense of identity and purpose for myself. This helps explain a lot of the bad choices I made while I was dating.

Please understand that *I* take full responsibility for the wrong life choices I made. *I* did those things to the ones I loved. *I* committed those sins. But I do want you to understand that the sins of others *can* damage our thought processes.

A Crisis Point and a Turning Point

When I married Alan, I did not understand how faulty my thinking was, and I had no idea it would eventually lead to trouble in our relationship. In the late 1990s, for various reasons, I had an affair. It lasted fourteen months. Alan was devastated and eventually, so was I. When he first began to suspect something, I denied it. When Alan discovered hard evidence of my behavior, I finally broke down and told him everything. He asked me to leave our home and to tell our two daughters why I was leaving.

Alan was pastor of a large church at this time and though he did not ask me to do it, I decided to face the congregation one Sunday morning and tell everyone what I had done. I knew that in order to break the power of my behavior and to truly have strength to change my ways, I had to be accountable, and I chose to be accountable to a *lot* of people that day.

Our church loved me and surrounded me, although many of them were angry with me because of how I had hurt Alan. The Robertson family had every reason to be furious with me, and they were deeply hurt over the way I had treated Alan, but after some time, they handled the situation in a godly way. I always tell people Miss Kay is a gentle person, and I know that maybe better than anyone.

Even though I caused her and the whole family great pain, she always treated me with gentleness during that terrible time.

In the aftermath of my confession, a special group of women spent time with me every evening and we studied the Bible and prayed for a new path for my life. One night after one of our group meetings, I was baptized in a friend's pool and felt relief and renewal and hope for the first time in a long, long time. The period of separation from Alan gave me a time of reflection that forced me to finally turn everything over to my Lord.

While Alan and I were apart, I lived with our next-door neighbors, who also happened to be our closest friends at the time and remain that way today. I went to their house so I could give Alan the space he needed and still take care of our home and our girls. Alan was not mean or ugly to me, but at the same time, he would not touch me or talk to me about anything except matters concerning the girls. I desperately wanted him to know what God was doing in my life, but I knew he did not trust me, so I kept a respectful distance.

TOGETHER AGAIN

One night Alan called me and asked me to meet him. I was afraid and excited at the same time. We talked a long time about reconciliation and what it would take to survive all the trauma our marriage had endured and to renew our relationship. By the end of the conversation, I was filled with hope, but I also knew that because Jesus had by then replaced Alan as the Lord of my life, I could survive no matter what happened with us.

At that time, I was seeing a wonderful counselor who was helping me through so much. After Alan and I talked that night, we started meeting with her together. I was learning that I had to forgive all of those who had sinned against me in my past (like the family member who abused me), and I was learning to build honesty and integrity into every decision I made. I learned that I did not exist to please men, but that God had created me with a unique and special purpose to please Him. I also learned to love God's Word in a whole new way, especially the Psalms and the Proverbs, which were my food during this deep look at myself. One of my new favorite verses was Proverbs 24:26, which says, "An honest answer is like a kiss on the lips." I determined that honesty with God, with myself, and with Alan was going to be one of my new character traits!

After about two months of being separated, Alan and I were reconciled. We renewed our vows to each other and bought new rings to signify our new beginning. We did not do any of this publicly, but just between ourselves, because we wanted it to be about God and about our starting something new and special. We continued our counseling together until we felt ready to begin a newly healed life and marriage.

STILL GOING STRONG

Alan and I are still going strong; we are more in love than ever and we have done our best to use the pain we have been through to help as many other people as we can. Our whole story is much longer and more complicated than I can share in this book. What I really want to communicate is that with God's help, a commitment to live by His Word, a loving family, a support system of fellow Christians, good counseling, and enough time, anything a person has been through can be healed, restored, and redeemed.

I have learned many valuable lessons during my life and in my journey as a Robertson—many of them the hard way through pain and difficulty. I can never say enough about how grateful I am that Alan and his family chose to forgive me, but one of the most important lessons I had to learn was to forgive myself. Without that, the forgiveness Alan, our daughters, our family, and our friends have extended to me would have been compromised. Had I never been able to forgive myself, I would have stayed stuck in my pain while others were moving on.

THERE IS HOPE FOR YOU

To people who have been through situations similar to mine, especially those who have experienced abuse or unfaithfulness on any level, I would say you can always come home to Christ. He is big enough to handle anything you have done or anything that has been done to you. His sacrifice on the cross is enough to cover anything.

Human beings can do a lot of bad things, but nothing you can do will cause Him to turn His back on you. No matter what has happened, refuse to live one more day as a victim. Know that Christ forgives you, and let that empower you to forgive yourself for even the biggest things.

I could spend every day of the rest of my life lamenting how much my past actions hurt the people I love. I refuse to do that because life is too short and because I know that God and the people around me want me to be healed and whole and strong, using everything that has happened in my life to encourage and support other people in their difficult times and to be the best wife, mother, and grandmother I can be.

I spent years doing the work I needed to do, with God's help and the support of great people, and now I can live in total freedom from the past. When talking about things like this, Miss Kay has a short but powerful piece of advice: "Confess it, own it, and move on." Sometimes that takes a while. Getting to the point where you have the courage to

Miss Kay has a short but powerful piece of advice: "Confess it, own it, and move on." —*Lisa*

confess may not happen overnight. Learning to own your thoughts, words, and actions may be a process. And you may have a few false starts before you get enough momentum to really move on. But even if it takes a while to work through your stuff, it's worth it. You, too, can ultimately end up in your very own happily ever after.

Part Four

TALKIN' ABOUT
MY GENERATIONS

Lord, You have been our dwelling place in all generations.

PSALM 90:1, NKJV

15

INTRODUCTION

A Message from the Wives

Our husbands grew up with the same parents and grandparents, but obviously, all of us became Robertsons later in life. We come from a variety of family experiences, all of which helped determine our values, shape our characters, and make us who we are today. Some of us have always enjoyed the kind of family closeness that characterizes the Robertsons; for others, coming into such a tight-knit family has been a blessing we did not have a chance to experience in our younger days.

We all understand the importance of generations and generational blessings. When we get together with Phil and Miss Kay and with our children and Lisa's grandchildren, we have four generations under the same roof. That family line is a powerful thread running through all of us as Robertsons. But intertwined with that thread is another thread for each of us, the generational heritage we bring from our own mothers and fathers, our grandparents, and other members of our extended families. It's amazing how all of this works together to weave a tapestry of love and faith in our lives and in the lives of our children.

16

AIN'T LIFE GRAND?

Miss Kay

When I think about the old saying "Ain't life grand?" I can't help but think about my *grand*mother, Nannie, and my *grand*children. All of these people have made my life grand indeed.

As a child, I lived near my grandparents, but not quite close enough to walk to their house easily. My family lived just down the road from my grandparents, and our family store was almost exactly halfway between the two houses. Our little town of about three hundred people, Ida, Louisiana, was located on the highway that runs between Texarkana and Shreveport, right about the half-way point, so a lot of traffic came through each day. The traffic was good for business in the store, but it meant no one would let me walk to my grandparents' house alone. Someone always had to take me or, when I got a little older, watch me cross the highway.

I spent a lot of time at my grandparents' house and loved every minute of it. It was a safe and happy place for me, and I look back on the years I spent with my grandparents as some of the best years of my life. One of my biggest regrets is that I did not record or write down many of the things my grandmother told me—the stories of her childhood, stories about her faith, and the simple words of wisdom she spoke as far back as I can remember. Like most young people, there was a time I thought I would never forget those things. There was also a time when I thought I would always have my grandparents. I could not imagine ever being without them, especially without my grandmother—but my grandfather died when I was twelve. Those people are gone now, and some of the memories are already getting a little fuzzy. I would give anything to be able to pull out a tape or a journal and relive them. I try to encourage people I know to take time to record or write down the things that are important to them, especially family stories and special memories, because a time will come when they will want to read or listen to them.

NANNIE AND ME

When I was growing up, in a small Southern town, the local store was not anything like the grocery stores or supermarkets of today. It was a gathering place. Life seemed to move more slowly than it does today, and people came to my daddy's store not only to buy their groceries but also to visit with their neighbors, talk about the news, and catch up on what was happening around town.

For as long as I can remember, I have loved and valued older people. Maybe that started during my days in the store. Especially in the wintertime, old women came to the store to sit around the heater. They were lonely (and cold), and the store was a hub of life and activity for them. I was a very social child, and I totally enjoyed visiting with the older people in our town. They called me "Little Katie Carroway," and I thought that was cute. I did my best to engage them in conversation or to entertain them with stories about my animals.

But there were no old people I loved like I loved my grandmother. In addition to sitting on the swing, waving at cars, and talking every evening, we did all kinds of other things together. For example, I had the cutest little black-and-white Shetland pony at my grandparents' house. His name was Tony, and he was so patient with me! I would ride him while my grandfather plowed, then Nannie would tie him to a tree and watch me do tricks while he just stood there and let me do whatever I wanted to do to him. In those days, I wanted to be just like Annie Oakley. I had a cowgirl outfit, and I would turn flips off of Tony. I had the time of my life with that little horse, and I think Nannie enjoyed it too.

Nannie had a pet too—a little fox terrier named Lady who *really* could do tricks. She could jump up in the air and do all kinds of things, even flips. Nannie and I were just crazy about that little dog. We never knew exactly where she came from but decided she must have been traveling with a family who stopped at the store and accidentally left her there. I cannot imagine anyone would have left behind such a good pet on purpose, especially in those days, but at least she went to a good home. Nannie kept Lady for the rest of that dog's life.

Nannie taught me all kinds of things about nature, such as the fact that there are "nice" caterpillars and "bad" caterpillars. I learned at an early age to tell the difference between the two and I collected as many nice ones as I could find. But I did not just collect them; I made a circus out of them! I had all kinds of little circuses when I was a child, using any kind of animal I could corral—earthworms, turtles, nice caterpillars, whatever I could find. Daddy always told me to stay away from skunks, and he would not let me touch squirrels, so most of my circus animals were small, but I just loved them.

One day, I put an entire circus of caterpillars in a box and took it to my daddy's store. The old people who sat around visiting with each other thought the circus and I were great entertainment. They thoroughly enjoyed it until all the caterpillars got loose. That was the end of my traveling circus, but I kept a circus of various types of animals at home and at my grandparents' house for years.

When I was not playing circus, I liked to play beauty shop, and Nannie never minded being my model. She had very thin hair, which she never cut—ever, not once in her whole life. It grew down her back to a certain point and then stopped. I remember many times when she sat patiently while I teased it, braided it, or put it up on top of her head. She also enjoyed sitting and watching me try on her hats, scarves, and jewelry while parading in front of the mirror.

One thing I really liked about my grandmother was that she was definitely *not* a neat freak. I am pretty sure I inherited that from her, and I think all my family would agree. No one could ever rightly accuse me of being too neat. I loved my grandmother's relaxed approach to everything and the fact that her house was often a little messy, because that made me feel at home. I never was afraid I would lose or mess up anything. I felt free to explore Nannie's house, play with her things, and let my imagination run wild.

My aunt Georgie visited my grandmother a lot and even though she was actually Nannie's sister, she called Nannie "Mother." She *was* a neat freak, and she had a habit of getting onto Nannie and me when I played with Nannie's nice things. I cannot even count the times I heard her say to Nannie, "Don't let Katie play with that!"

Nannie had a set of beautiful demitasse cups I used to play tea party. No one was there, of course, but I liked to pretend I had a group of friends around me and all of us were drinking tea from Nannie's special cups. That especially got on Aunt Georgie's nerves. One day, as usual, she saw me playing tea party with the cups and said to Nannie, "Don't let her play with those. They are expensive and they are nice, and she will break them."

> I felt free to explore Nannie's house, play with her things, and let my imagination run wild.
> —*Miss Kay*

I knew the cups were special, and I was very careful with them. I felt so good that day when Nannie responded to Aunt Georgie, "Number one, she would only break something by accident. She would not do it on purpose. And number two, those cups are just things, and people are more important than things." Nannie knew how much fun I had at my tea parties and my having a good time was much more important to her than making sure nothing got broken.

I am so glad my grandmother felt the way she did about her things. She always kept her possessions in perspective, and I had hours of enjoyment at her house because she was that way. I try to be the same way with my grandchildren. I do not want them coming to my house and being afraid I will get upset if they break something. Over the years, society has put so much emphasis on stuff—

having nice stuff and getting more stuff. We have become a culture of accumulation and "What about me?" I never heard those kinds of things growing up. People worked hard to get what they needed and wanted; they took care of what belonged to them and they shared with others in need. People were not so focused on getting more and more stuff.

I wish we had not lost that attitude and generous spirit in our country because it was a very good way to live. In recent years, with 9/11, we have seen that many people still have the ability to reach out, pull together, share with others, and think about others. A tragedy will almost always help people return to the things that really matter. But I am afraid we have lost our ability to be content and to care for others, and I wish we could get it back.

SOMEONE'S IN THE KITCHEN WITH NANNIE

As I mentioned earlier, my grandmother *always* seemed to be cooking. She was often the first person in our community to take food to people who had sickness or a death in their family. I saw her do that often while I was growing up, and other ladies in the community did the same. If a family lost a loved one or was dealing with an illness, they hardly ever had to think about what they would eat. The women of the town provided for them. Taking food to people in need was a way of showing them you cared about them and about what they were going through. That doesn't seem to happen much anymore; people do not reach out to others as much as they used to. Back then, food was a way of showing love, and for me, it still is.

These days I try to teach my grandchildren about cooking and to pass on my love for cooking to them. Cooking is not something I do because our family has to eat; it's something I do because I thoroughly enjoy it. My love for cooking started in childhood in my grandmother's kitchen, and now I want my grandchildren to learn to love cooking in my kitchen. They love my biscuits, and if they don't learn anything else, they will learn how to make those! If you want to learn to make them, too, the recipe is in the section of this book called "Inquiring Minds Want to Know" and also in my cookbook entitled *Miss Kay's Duck Commander Kitchen*.

Fun Times Together

My grandchildren are always eager to hear stories about my childhood, whether I talk about being in the kitchen with Nannie, doing tricks on Tony, or loving the old people at the store. They are interested in stories about their fathers when they were young. I sometimes rely on Alan to talk about those days because he has a great memory and remembers a lot of things I have forgotten. They also love to hear about the things Nannie and I used to do together. I try to do with them some of the same things I did with her years ago, and we also do new things I have thought of recently.

I love to laugh with my grandchildren. I want them to have fun with me, and I try to make just about everything an adventure. One day I decided to take them to visit Phil's sister, who lives just over the hill and through the woods from Phil and me. There is a well-worn trail Phil and I normally take to her house, but that day I thought I would give the children a little adventure by taking a different route. I led the way down an overgrown path that was completely covered with vines. We almost felt like we were pioneering through an African jungle. The children loved it, and I thought it was fun, too, until I got so tangled up in a bunch of vines I literally could not move. I didn't want to frighten them, so I started laughing and crying, "Help me! Help me!" very dramatically. To this day, the children have no idea I was *really* stuck. I truly could not get out of those vines. I was laughing so hard they thought I was kidding. Thankfully, someone came to my house while I was all tied up, heard us laughing in the distance, and came to my rescue. Now *that* was an adventure, and the kids just love to laugh and retell it.

My adventurous spirit is something that has grown in me over the years. I certainly was not born with it. My sister seemed to get all the adventure genes in the family, while I was more like Chicken Little. Except for doing tricks on my pony, which some people would say takes bravery, the most adventurous thing I ever did as a child was to skip one class while others skipped a whole day of school. They thought playing hooky would be so much fun, but I was afraid to do it. While they were out having fun, I decided to hide behind the Coke machine during one class period. It was no fun at all! I was bored and scared I would get caught. Over the years, maybe from living with a man as adventurous as Phil, I have learned to look for adventure and embrace it, especially when the grandchildren are around.

Sometimes, when we have had enough adventures for a while, we play a quiet little game called the Listening Game. I say to the children, "Close your eyes, and just *listen*." The children sit for a few seconds and say they do not hear anything. I tell them to keep

> My adventurous spirit is something that has grown in me over the years. I certainly was not born with it. —*Miss Kay*

listening. Eventually the children hear different kinds of birds, frogs, squirrels, and other animals—even a woodpecker pecking on a nearby tree. By the time the game is over, they are delighted with the sounds of the outdoors.

THE GREATEST STORY OF ALL

I love being able to spend time with my grandchildren and having fun with them. I am so thankful for the things we can do together and the good times we enjoy. I am glad they are interested in the stories I tell, but there is one story I want to make sure they know better than all the rest. It's the story that determines everything else about their lives, the story of Jesus.

When I talk to the children about Jesus, I use a simple illustration of symbols across a page. You can see it in my own handwriting on the dedication page of this book. A downward-pointing arrow means, "Jesus came." In other words, He gave up everything wonderful about heaven and came to live on earth, where everything is not always wonderful. He came as a regular boy and grew to be a man. The next symbol looks like a large "plus" sign, but it's really a cross and it means, "Jesus died." He died for all of our sins. The next symbol looks kind of like an extended letter "n," and it represents the tomb where Jesus' body lay for three days after His death. The next symbol is an upward-pointing arrow, which means Jesus ascended to heaven. The final symbol is another downward-pointing arrow, representing the promise that Jesus will one day return to earth and take us back to heaven with Him if we have trusted Him as our Lord and Savior.

When my boys were little, I made sure each one knew this story as soon as he was old enough to understand it. Now I do the same with my grandchildren. Sometimes, just to reinforce the power of the story, I talk to them about Jesus' crucifixion and say, "All those people treated Jesus so well. They took Him out to eat and bought His dinner . . ." Someone, usually Mia, quickly interrupts with, "No, Mamaw Kay! They *didn't*! They put real nails and thorns in His hands—and thorns *hurt*."

I like to explain to the children that no one gets buried in a tomb today, at least not where we live. As I talk about that, the children like to envision what a dark, musty tomb would have been like. When we talk about the tomb, we talk about dying and going to heaven. Then we talk about how a person's spirit goes to heaven when he or she dies and then gets reunited with the body when Jesus comes back. And we talk about the fact that while we are living here on earth, we can talk to God any time we want, knowing He is always listening when we pray.

When Phil is around and I am reminding the children of the Gospel story, he waits for me to get to the part about Jesus' ascending back to heaven and inserts, very intensely, "He probably went up *just like a rocket ship!*" They are fascinated by that thought. I don't know if it was really like a rocket ship or not, but it makes a great visual for little ones. I love to talk to my grandchildren about Jesus and to ask them questions to make sure they understand this awesome story. They do.

I am confident they know and believe the truth of the Gospel, and I am thankful they all have parents who also make a priority of telling this story in their homes and of taking the children to church so they can learn even more about God.

The grandchildren also like to hear other stories from the Bible, and I enjoy reminding them of these stories that so many generations of people, including me, grew up on. Their favorites are the ones about God's miracles or other things that really stand out, such as Jonah and the whale or Balaam and the talking donkey. Of course, all of us Robertsons love animals, so we tell the story of Noah and the ark. I take every opportunity I have to remind the children of these stories because I want to make sure they never lose sight of everything God has done and everything God can do. I know the children understand because I sometimes hear them retelling the stories in their own words, and their versions are so sweet.

I love the innocence and faith the younger grandchildren have, and I hope they never lose it. I also love the boldness and faith the older ones are developing. They just amaze me. When they have opportunities to speak, they do not shy away from sharing their faith. They are bold about it, and I am so proud of them for standing up for what they believe.

USE YOUR IMAGINATION

When I was a child, there were no such things as cell phones or electronic games. I always wanted to be outside with Tony the pony or with my circus, so I was not the type of person to sit inside and move little things around on a screen. I would not have sat in a chair texting people because I wanted to be at the store interacting personally with the people of our community. I understand how helpful technology can be, but I do not want it taking over my time with my grandchildren, so the little ones know they cannot bring their phones or latest gadgets to my house. When they're with me, we do artsy-crafty projects, we collect interesting things from nature, and we talk about how unique they are and how God created them.

One day when we were outside, Lily caught a granddaddy longlegs. It was harmless of course, but where we live we also have black widows and brown recluses, which are *not* harmless! I asked her to let the granddaddy longlegs go, but she did not really want to. I explained that the younger children in the family were watching her and even though she knew the difference between harmless and dangerous spiders, they did not. She understood right away and did not want to set a bad example for them. That did not stop her from catching a garden snake a few weeks later, though!

I will never forget my circus and when I think about it these days, I realize being able to do that and to have some encouragement from my family in it really helped me develop my own curiosity and imagination. I try to revisit that with my granddaughters and River because I think imagination is a lost art in modern society. Any time I can encourage the children to be creative and to use their imaginations, I do.

One of my favorite little happy things to do is to give the children prizes—not anything expensive, just something that communicates, "I was thinking of you." Sometimes, River loses his prize while he is at my house. When I find it, I give it back to him, and he thinks it's new. I am not sure how long that will last (at the time of this writing he is only five years old), but I am going to make the most of it while it does.

LICKETY SPLIT

Phil and I have several small buildings on our property, many of which were used for Duck Commander at one time. In one of those buildings close to our house, I made my granddaughters a little playhouse called the Lickety Split. It's just for the girls because little girls have certain things they really like to do. It's just precious what they are into. For example, my granddaughters like to have a play office and a place to do little performances. In 2013, I hired some decorators to improve the Lickety Split. They created a stage and place to sit, and put in a karaoke machine, a keyboard, and a microphone. They also installed a play kitchen they call a bistro. In another part of the room, there is an old dresser where the girls can do their hair and play dress-up. The ladies did a great job with it; it's darling.

As much as I appreciated the decorators' talents, I was most excited about the fact that once they finished their work, the girls took over. They made it their own. They do some things the decorators might call "messing up their work," but that's not the case. The girls are simply creative, and like most children, they want to put their stamp on things. I was happy to help create the Lickety Split for them and do my best to make it something they can enjoy, but I was even happier to see them use their imaginations and make it even more of what they wanted it to be.

I Love Them All

All of my grandchildren are a blessing. They are all different and all special. They seem to trust me, and I treasure that. I would not trade their trust for anything in this whole wide world. I enjoy them so much, and one of these days, say, when they are my age, I want them to really know and understand just how much I loved them. I hope they will always think of me as a fun grandmother who loved to laugh and as a positive influence in their lives. I want to be someone who teaches them about life and faith and about right and wrong. I want to be to them everything my grandmother was to me, and more. I'm working on it every day. I do not want them to think of me as a cranky ol' grumbling grandmother; I like to say I want to be a sunshine grandma.

I know Korie's grandmother, and I know Jessica's grandmother, both lovely women. When I look at Korie and Jessica, they both have so many of the qualities I see in their grandmothers, especially their sweetness and humility. In years to come, I hope people who have known me will know my grandchildren and be able to say, "She got that from Miss Kay," or "He's that way because of what Miss Kay taught him." Most of all, I want them to grow up to be people who love and obey God, love their families, and know the difference between right and wrong. I pray I am a godly influence and a blessing in their lives, just as they are in mine.

17

A LEGACY OF LOVE

Jessica

I grew up as part of a large extended family, and a lot of our family gatherings took place at my grandparents' house. I have such happy memories of being at their house with my aunts, uncles, and cousins. As a child, I was a tomboy, and I climbed trees and rode four-wheelers with my cousins. I also remember being so excited to get to go with my mamaw Nellie and papaw Ted (my mom's parents) to their garden and pick vegetables. Some of my favorite times were when our entire family gathered for a big feast after church on Sundays, the same kind of large meals Miss Kay prepares for the Robertson clan today.

These memories, and the fact that I grew up around such hard-working, faith-filled, wonderful people, are part of the reason I grew up loving my family. For years, I never really thought people lived any other way. Not spending time with family was never an option for us. Now I am sad when I think about people who did not have that kind of upbringing or children who are not able to experience the blessings of a close-knit family. Don't get me wrong, no one is perfect and no one's life is perfect. My family had struggles just like any other family, but we loved each other unconditionally—and unconditional love never gives up on anyone. We stood by each other, and when one member of the family felt broken, the others helped lift that one up. The same is true in the Robertson family; no one views himself or herself as better than anyone else. We all love each other and want each other to succeed.

I WAS MEANT TO BE A ROBERTSON

Sometimes I think I was always destined to be a Robertson because I come from a family full of hunters and fishermen—on both sides. One of my grandfathers, Papaw Ted, worked in a chicken plant to make a living and had a hunting camp as a hobby.

My other grandfather, Papaw James, and grandmother, Mamaw Lola, had a fishing camp. I remember lots of lazy summer days when the men in our family went fishing early in the mornings and the rest of us swam and soaked ourselves in the sun until they got back. When they returned, we all took the boat out again for an afternoon of water skiing, tubing, and knee-boarding. At night, we fried the morning's catch for dinner and always had delicious meals because both of my grandmothers were great cooks.

> Sometimes I think I was always destined to be a Robertson because I come from a family full of hunters and fishermen.
>
> —*Jessica*

When I think back to my growing-up days with my extended family, I also remember being so excited as a little girl, at early elementary school age, when I went hunting with my dad, my uncles, and my grandfather. On those cold mornings, they let me drink coffee with lots of cream and sugar. That was a real treat, and I loved it!

Both of my grandfathers, my uncles, and my dad were all outdoorsmen, so part of my generational legacy is part of Jep's legacy too. We both come from people who know how to bait hooks and load rifles—and how to clean and eat what they kill. Both of our families include careful, responsible hunters and fishermen who understand nature and the life cycles that take place in it. They know how to respect and work within the natural order of things.

I also come from a line of women who know how to garden and how to cook—not just cook, but how to cook *really* well. In the South, that is important! I love and appreciate my family so much, and I am thankful for the great family experiences I had growing up.

Like me, Jep also loves all of his family and is very loyal to them. He had especially good relationships with Granny and Pa. Because they lived so close to Phil and Miss Kay when Jep was a little boy, he stayed with them a lot while Miss Kay was busy working. In fact, Granny taught Jep how to bait a fishhook and how to play hearts and gin rummy. Miss Kay likes to talk about the fact that Granny and Pa taught the boys how to play dominoes, which really helped them with their math skills. Now she is a lot like they were because she loves combining play and fun things with learning opportunities. Both Granny and Pa taught Jep and his brothers a lot of important lessons about life, which they still remember and are passing on to their own children.

Our daughter Merritt is named after Granny. When all the grandchildren were born, Granny made each of them an afghan. When she found out Merritt was her namesake, she made Merritt two!

THE VALUE OF FAMILY

Jep and I are doing our best to teach our children the importance of spending time with family. We understand the value of the generations and want our children to know and love their grandparents the way we knew and loved ours, so we try to make sure they see their grandparents several times a week. I sometimes hear about people who do not get along well with their in-laws, and they hinder their children's relationships with their grandparents. This always makes me sad because I believe grandparents add so much to children's lives and that young people suffer when they cannot be around their grandparents. The love of a grandmother is different from the love of a mother; the same is true for fathers and grandfathers, and children can really benefit from all the generations before them.

Most Wednesdays Miss Kay takes the girls to Outback or Cracker Barrel and then to Hobby Lobby for little prizes or trinkets. She also takes them to libraries and reads to them. And, of course, she lets them check out books from "their" library at her house.

I want my children to spend as much time as possible with all of their grandparents. My parents have something special to offer them, just as Phil and Miss Kay do. I believe the children need to hear stories about Miss Kay's hard times and they need to learn from Phil how to get along in the woods. They even need to know Uncle Si went to Vietnam and risked his life for the freedom they now enjoy.

OUR DREAMS COME TRUE

The children also need time with Jep and me and with each other. Jep and I really make an effort to have family night with our children at least once a week. Jep and I both always wanted a large family; that was something we talked about and dreamed of before we married. Now we have been blessed with four awesome children.

Lily, our oldest daughter, has always been so sweet and loves everyone. She was born in 2002 and went through a lot of illness during the first few years of her life, including a weeklong hospital stay for rotavirus when she was two years old. Through all her illnesses, she remained the sweetest little girl, not crying or fussing very much, even though I know she was uncomfortable.

Lily has always been quiet, and she gets that from Jep, not from me. I am definitely a talker! Lily is shy, but she is also smart and hardworking, and she makes good grades in school. She loves babies and music. In fact, not long before I started writing this book, she started taking mandolin lessons. She also has good athletic abilities, and whether she is playing a sport, doing her homework, or doing something else, she gives 100 percent. I love Lily's sweet spirit and the way she loves everyone.

Merritt is our second child and second daughter. She was my hardest baby and literally cried almost all the time; but she is a surprisingly easy child. She is strong, spunky, and independent. Like her dad, she does not feel the need for other people's approval (I am much more of a people pleaser). Because Merritt does not make decisions based on what other people think, she is really good at choosing friends. She decides whether or not to be friends with people based on their character and personality, not based on whether they are considered "popular." I love the confidence I see in her. Merritt is a talented singer and pianist, and she took up the guitar not long before I started writing this book. She is also a pretty good golfer, and Jep is really glad about that!

Priscilla is our third child and third daughter. Of all our children, Priscilla looks the most like Jep. Her baby pictures are almost identical to his. She is definitely our sassiest child! She is extremely competitive, yet she is also very sweet, and she loves to hug and give kisses. Physically speaking, she is tough, and she does not recognize her own strength. Because of her strength and toughness, I will not be surprised if she excels in sports someday. Priscilla is also very girly. She loves to wear dresses, curl her hair, and play with baby dolls. She also plays the piano and takes fiddle lessons. Jep says I baby her more than the others, and I just say, "Well, she will always be my baby girl."

Our fourth child and only boy is River. He is the last of the Robertson grandchildren and the last of Jep's and my children, so I have to admit he gets a little spoiled. He is such a cutie, with Jep's dark hair and blue eyes, and those famous Robertson dimples! At the time of this writing, River is five years old. I know he will have another leading lady in his life someday, but for now I am enjoying this time when he wants his mama more than anyone else. He is "a lover and a fighter." He loves on me all the time, but he also gets physical with his sisters over something on a daily basis. He can be a little stinker in that way, but he really loves his sisters. I know that being around all these girls will help him be a better husband one day.

THE PRIORITY OF FAMILY TIME

With our busy schedules, family time together is not always easy for us, but it is important, so we try to prioritize it even if we have to sacrifice other things. "Family night" means different things at different times; the only requirement is that we spend time together as a family. Sometimes, we all cook and eat outside together. Then Jep and I watch the children play and light the fire pit so we can end the evening with s'mores. Sometimes we play games or watch good, clean, wholesome movies.

On some family nights, Jep and I teach the children a Bible lesson because we know how valuable God's Word is and how much it can help them in life. We want them to know what it says and to be able to understand what it means so they can apply it in their lives, even at their young ages.

As often as possible, whether it's family night or not, Jep and I cook dinner for the children. Well, actually, Jep prepares the meals and I clean up. I absolutely love the fact that my man can cook! Two of our favorite family activities are playing Monopoly and making the kids' all-time favorite dessert, homemade snow cones. Several times a week, Jep takes the kids outside to hit golf balls and they have so much fun doing it. Jep has fun, too, but I am pretty sure he secretly wants one of them to turn pro!

Recently, we came up with an idea for an activity that has had such a positive impact on our family. We give everyone a chance to draw a word out of a hat. Every word in the hat comes from Galatians 5:22–23, a scripture passage that refers to "the fruit of the Spirit," meaning the qualities of a person whose life is filled with and led by God's Holy Spirit. It says: "The fruit of the Spirit is love, joy, peace, patience, kindness, goodness, faithfulness, gentleness, and self-control."

We have nine words in the hat, and we draw one each week. I post the word on the refrigerator, and it becomes the character quality we all work on for the next seven days. Let me tell you, my children do not forget what we are working on that week, because when one of them does not display that particular fruit, the others will let him or her know. I can't count the times I've heard someone say, "You are not being patient with me," or "Remember, we're supposed to be working on kindness this week, and you are not being kind!"

Like any mom, I would really like for each person to work on his or her own fruit before pointing out someone else's shortcoming, but I have to say: it works!

In our family, we make it a point to pray together as much as we can. I believe some of the sweetest prayers ever prayed come from children, because they are so pure-hearted, so innocent, and so full of faith. As a mom, I just love to hear them talk to God, and of course, I love it when they see the answers to their prayers.

Family—and everything family means to us—is the legacy Jep and I want to leave our children. A big part of that legacy is a commitment to faith and love. My parents have lived that way and so have my grandparents. That's what I have seen in them, and that's what I want our children to see in Jep and me. If they do, we will have succeeded. And if Jep and I can raise children who live according to the fruit of the Spirit, know and obey God's Word, pray, and love their family, we will have accomplished something very fulfilling, and we will have given them the foundation they need in order to build great lives in the future.

18

JUST CALL ME MAM

Lisa

I am so glad Miss Kay and my sisters-in-law have happy memories with their grandparents. My memories are less pleasant, simply because my grandparents' house was the place where a member of my extended family abused me for years. Even though I spent a lot of time there, much of it was filled with fear and pain. But my grandmother was a very sweet lady, and my mother tells me I received some of my physical attributes from her. If you wonder what I mean, let me get specific: hips and rear!

My grandmother and I spent a lot of time together during my childhood, and when I stayed with her, she took me fishing about three times a week. That is how I learned to spit, potty in the woods, and bait a hook. Those times with her were also where I gained my love for fishing with a cane pole. She could slap that thing down in the water like nobody's business! When she took me fishing, we caught bream and then went home to scrape 'em, clean 'em, and eat 'em.

My grandmother also let me help her in her garden, and I still love to shell peas and shuck corn because of her influence. I spent a lot of time with my grandmother; I do not fault her for the choices my relative made, but my memories sometimes get a little skewed when I think of my childhood with her.

My biological family has endured a lot of sadness and hardship over the years, so sometimes looking back is difficult. I lost my father to cancer, my sister and brother to alcoholism, a nephew to a motorcycle accident, and many aunts, uncles, and cousins for different reasons. I am the only child left to my mother. She has really been through a lot of heartache, but she has endured, and we are held together by our mother-daughter bond and Christ's love. She is very strong and opinionated, and Alan will quickly say I received that trait from her.

I don't blame my parents for what happened in my childhood. They didn't know! When I did tell my mother about it, she confronted our relative, but he denied it or said he didn't "remember doing that." I have told her it has been dealt with and Christ has healed me. She was glad for that news, at least.

My mother has found joy in keeping my grandchildren while Alan and I work, and they share a close relationship with her. Even though thinking about my past is difficult, thinking about the family I have with Alan and looking forward—now *that's* a different story. When I think about the generations in our family, the people who bring me the most joy are my daughters and grandchildren. I believe our daughters, our sons-in-law, and our grandchildren have a bright future built on a strong relationship with God, and that gives me great hope for the days ahead.

Earlier in the book I wrote about the troubles Alan and I faced at one period in our marriage. There was a time when we both wondered whether we would still be together all these years later, and we thank God we are. I want to pick up that story now where I left off.

I was only eighteen years old when Alan and I married, and as I mentioned, we spent the early days of our marriage living with Granny and Pa on Phil and Miss Kay's property. As a young wife, I had great role models in Granny and Miss Kay. In fact, Miss Kay taught me some lessons in those early years that saved my marriage to Alan later on. I learned from her to fight for my marriage. Though her troubles with Phil were different from the problems Alan and I went through, she had a level of commitment to her husband and her marriage I had never seen before. I knew she had been through extremely difficult times and refused to let them get the best of her. I also noticed how genuinely loving and respectful she was toward Phil. She never held anything against him. When she forgave, she forgave completely, and that laid the groundwork for the wonderful marriage she and Phil have today. She taught me how to love, especially how to love Alan, and even though I seemed to abandon those lessons for a while, I now put them to good use every day. As a young bride, I had no idea how powerful those things I learned from her would be for me, but I thank God I learned them.

THE TABLE: MORE THAN JUST A PIECE OF FURNITURE

One of the best things about those years was the time our family spent together around the table. Robertsons are people who value the family table, not just because it's filled with some of the best food on earth, but because it provides a place for conversation, storytelling, talking about the day, and sometimes a spirited disagreement—which all help build strong family relationships. When Alan and I lived on Phil and Miss Kay's property, the whole family ate together almost every night. Miss Kay usually did most of the cooking, but Granny and I pitched in a little. Granny and I took our food up the hill to Phil and Miss Kay's house, and we all sat down to eat together. Occasionally, when Miss Kay was too busy to cook, Granny prepared our meals and we all went to her and Pa's house to eat.

In many parts of our society today, the family table has disappeared and a lot of people have lost something vital in family relationships because of it. When I was young, and even after I was married, everyone ate what was served and we ate when it was ready. Children did not eat alone in front of the television or in their rooms with a fork in one hand and a cell phone in the other. Families actually sat together, prayed together, and talked as they shared their meal. Around the table, people knew they had a place where they belonged, a place to disagree and still be loved, a place to talk about what was going on in their lives, and a safe place to learn relational skills. I believe that concept of the family table is one of many values of the past that contributed to strong families, which in turn made strong communities and built a strong nation.

In our family, we still value the table, and I know many others do too. I am thankful for that, because I believe it is so important. It certainly is for us, and it always has been. It is one part of what makes us Robertsons who we are.

> Around the table, people knew they had a place where they belonged. —*Lisa*

A NEW GENERATION OF ROBERTSONS

Within the first five years of my marriage to Alan, we had two daughters, Anna and Alex. Anna was born prematurely, at twenty-nine weeks. She was twelve inches long and weighed one pound, fifteen ounces. The first several months of Anna's life, she lived in the neonatal intensive care unit and underwent serious heart surgery. Alan and I were filled with fear and uncertainty, not sure whether she would live or not.

Thankfully, Anna survived and soon became a happy baby. Miss Kay had taught me how to cook when Alan and I were first married, and she taught me how to be a mother after Anna was born. I don't know what I would have done without her and Granny!

After raising four boys, Miss Kay was so excited to have a little girl in the family. When Anna was born, Miss Kay bought paper dolls, Barbies, hair bows, dress-up clothes—anything she could think of that was girlie. Even though she had to wait a while before Anna was old enough to play with some of those things, Miss Kay had them ready. She and Anna are still extremely close. I learned early in their relationship something I missed in my own childhood—the legacy of having grandmothers and being able to learn from them is amazing.

Anna was strong-willed as a child but became very mild-mannered and compliant as a teenager. Some people might say that could never happen, but it did. The opposite happened with our daughter Alex. She was an easygoing child but followed a more typical pattern when she reached her teenage years and became rebellious and stubborn.

At age eighteen, in a decision that really disappointed Alan and me, Alex was doing some things we did not approve of and decided to move away from home. Alan and I loved her but did not think she had made a wise decision. However, we did not see any wisdom in trying to force her to do what we wanted her to do. We refused to take away her power of choice. We hoped and prayed she would come to realize her mistakes on her own and choose to do differently. We were always there for her when she wanted guidance and we gave her good advice. Then we waited for her to decide what to do with that advice and to figure out how she wanted to live her life.

Several years later, I received the following note from Alex.

. . . I just wanted to tell you how much I love you and admire you. Sometimes when I was younger, we didn't get along because I didn't understand why you wouldn't just let me do what I wanted to do! But now I see that you did everything because you love me and you wanted me to stay out of trouble! I am glad you have become not only my mom, but one of my very best friends as well. When I think of the perfect mom, I think of you. I have so much respect for you now that I am old (and wise) enough to

see all of the great, wonderful qualities in you. My admiration
for you tripled when I heard your full testimony in Africa. To be
able to go through all the things you have gone through and still
come out a loving, godly, sparkling, shining example of what a
woman should be is very inspiring. I hope I wind up just like you
some day! I love you and Daddy with all my heart!

Today, Alex has graduated from culinary school, and she is a fabulous cook. She and her husband, Vinny, live close to Alan and me in West Monroe, and our relationship with her is completely restored.

THE SPECIAL GIFT OF GRANDCHILDREN

Because of choices I made when our daughters were young and what they lived through during the time Alan and I were apart, I have told them, "I may not have been the best mother and I'm sorry, but I promise I am going to be a *great* grandmother to your children." I work toward that goal every day.

I have learned a lot about being a grandmother from Miss Kay, and she is exactly the kind of grandmother I want to be. She is just great with all of her grandchildren. They all think she is so much fun and they love her dearly. She is such an encourager to everyone, and she definitely encourages her grandsons and grand-daughters in every way she can. She makes an effort to spend as much time with them as possible, and that has not been easy since *Duck Dynasty* started. But she works hard to arrange time with them. She teaches the girls how to cook, she plays Barbies, she sings in the car, and she has created an outright fun masterpiece with the Lickety Split.

At the time of this writing, Alan and I have two granddaughters. Anna and her husband, Jay, are the happy parents of Carley, who was born in 2005, and Bailey, born in 2007. Alex and her husband, Vinny, are expecting our third grandchild. It will be our first grandson in March.

Our grandchildren are such an awesome blessing. Being a grandparent is completely different from being a parent, and Alan and I love it! Of course, we think our granddaughters are adorable and fun. Like many grandparents, we think our granddaughters are the cutest little girls who ever lived. And they are. But for Alan and me, the granddaughters are so much more than cute. They are an amazing symbol of God's restoration and healing power. When we think back on our years of doubt, heartache, and possible divorce, we realize that our lives—and the lives of our children and grandchildren—would be totally different had we not made the choices we made. Had we decided not to stay together, we would not be able to do any of the fun things we do together now. We would not take our granddaughters on trips (which we do as often as possible), and we would not enjoy having them spend the night with us (sometimes multiple nights in a row) or special holiday times together. Our grandchildren would have to visit us in separate homes and miss the togetherness and security of being surrounded by the extended family into which they were born. Personally, I realize I would also have missed the joy of knowing my Robertson nieces and nephews. Had Alan and I divorced, generations of Robertsons would have suffered. Because God gave us the grace to tough it out, and because Alan forgave me and the Robertsons embraced me again after I had failed, our whole family is happy together. It was not easy, but was *definitely* worth it. I believe our grandchildren are God's gift to Alan and me because we did not give up. We love spending time with them. We deeply love both of our daughters, but we both agree—as most grandparents would—that God has given us something special in our grandchildren.

When the time came for Alan and me to decide what we wanted our grandchildren to call us, we landed on Mam and Pap. The parents in a book I read years ago used these names and I always liked them, so I started calling myself Mam, and it stuck. When our granddaughters were learning to say "yes, ma'am" and "no, ma'am," "yes, sir" and "no, sir," they did fine with Alan, but when they spoke to me, they had to say, "Yes, ma'am, Mam." They still say that, and it is so cute.

> Because God gave us the grace to tough it out, and because Alan forgave me, our whole family is happy together. —*Lisa*

As much as Alan and I love our grandchildren, we want our daughters and sons-in-law to be their parents. We do not want to overstep parental boundaries. We want to influence in the right ways, but we do not want to take on roles that are not appropriate for us. When the grandchildren make a mess at our house, we insist they clean it up, but we do not discipline them in ways that are better left to their parents.

Alan and I also let our grandchildren know they can tell us anything. I stress this point because of my past. I tell them there are no secrets between them and Mam. I even go so far as to talk about appropriate touches and who should touch them, and where it is okay for them to be touched. I also tell them that no matter what they tell Pap and me, we will *never* stop loving them. We want them to know, as we know and our daughters know, that we are family and we do *not* give up on one another. Because of our story, that really means something.

A HERITAGE OF FAITH

Korie

I come from a long line of people who value faith and family, just as the Robertsons do. From both my dad's side, the Howards, and my mom's side, the Shackelfords, my children and I have a generational heritage of dedicated Christians who loved the Lord, loved others, and made a big difference for God in the world around them. I am thankful for that legacy and enjoy seeing specific traits that have been passed down to our children and are helping shape them into the individuals they are today and will become in the future.

OUR OWN LITTLE FAMILY

John Luke is our firstborn. When I think of him, the first word that comes to mind is "adventurer." He loves to meet new people and will stop by a tent revival or county fair on the side of the road in a heartbeat. He is the first to stop and pull a truck out of a ditch or give money to someone in need. When he was a little boy, he often made elaborate maps of the woods around our house and loved to take off on his own little explorations. Whatever he is doing and in whatever circumstance, he is happy. For as long as I can remember, every time I ask him how his day was his response has always been, "*Great!*"

John Luke sees the good in life and in others. Like his dad, he is fun to be around and is quite the romantic. He loves to make others smile and plan little surprises that will make the ones he loves happy—whether that's a friend, his girlfriend, or even his mom.

John Luke is a passionate follower of Christ. I could not have been more proud than when I looked at the "Notes" section on his iPhone and found page after page of Bible studies, favorite verses, and notes he had taken from lessons at church. John Luke believes he can change the world. He doesn't make the excuse that since he is a teenager he is supposed to "sow his wild oats" and rebel against his parents. He's out to make a difference, and he will. Not that he's never irresponsible or carefree; trust me, he's still a teenager. He has fun, is the first to jump up and get the party started, is always planning his next practical joke, and sometimes borrows Willie's truck and brings it back on empty.

Sadie is our second-born. She is funny and kind and thoughtful. When she was a child Willie nicknamed her "the Original." He said there has never been one like her and never will be.

Sadie keeps us laughing with her imitations of people in the family, her friends, and her teachers. She loves to sing and dance and is great at sports. I really haven't found anything she can't do.

She thinks about others' feelings and seems to always know when someone needs a little encouragement. She is always there to give it through a note, a hug, or a kind word. She does certain things with each of her siblings that make them feel special, and I could not be more proud of the way our children love each other and care for one another. Sadie makes sure this happens.

Sadie loves God with all her heart, and this was evident even when she was a young child. We have a video of her "preaching" at about five years old. Standing on the coffee table in our living room, she says, "It doesn't matter if you are a policeman or a jail person, God loves you. He wants you to be in heaven with Him."

We watched this video recently and were amazed at the insight Sadie had at such a young age. She even went on to say, "Even if I become famous one day, I will not just love myself. I will not forget about the Lord, 'cause I know He loves me and He is there for me." Wow! What wisdom and thoughtfulness from a five-year-old! She finished her speech with a cheer—"Let's give it up for God!"—in the cutest singsong voice. Yep, she's original, all right.

Will came next. He may not have grown in my stomach, but he certainly grew in my heart. Willie and I dreamed of and prayed for him from the time we were dating and knew we wanted to adopt a child someday. As soon as we saw a picture of this precious baby boy, we knew he was ours.

Will has a way of capturing the heart of everyone he meets. He makes friends in the toy section of Walmart, on the beach playing in the sand, and in the video game room at the pizza place. He has a great smile and a contagious laugh, and he remembers the name of everyone he meets. Even as a little boy he would say hi to the older ladies at church and call them by name. They were so impressed that he knew their names; they would gush over just how special he is, and I would agree.

Will is a people person and a family guy. He loves his siblings, his cousins, and, of course, his mom and dad, and he gives the best hugs to all. He's also got some special talents; he can beat-box and dance "Gangnam Style" like nobody's business. He was born with a beat in his head. As a baby he played the drums on his high chair and now can sit down at his drum set and pick out a beat at the drop of a hat. He also has a beautiful singing voice, which I know he will someday use for God. I could not be more proud of the man Will is becoming and can't wait to see what God has in store for him in the future.

> **Will makes friends in the toy section of Walmart, on the beach playing in the sand, and in the video game room at the pizza place.**
> —*Korie*

Bella is the baby of the family, but just barely. She was born when Will was only ten months old. Willie and I had always planned on having four children, so we knew we wanted one more baby after we adopted Will, but we were surprised when she came so soon. And Bella's been surprising us ever since. She has a fun, quirky, strong spirit. At three weeks old, she contracted salmonella. She was in the hospital for a week, but it took months before her little digestive system recovered. She was a tough little cookie then and she still is now.

I have always said Bella was born knowing what she wants and where she is going. From the moment she could walk and talk, she would just take off, and you knew you'd better keep up! At just three years old, she loved to place her own order at the drive-through. She would stick her head out the window and say in her cute little-girl voice, "I'll have chicken nuggets and a Dr Pepper, with *no* ice." When she was about five years old she sat on Santa's lap and told him she wanted Dr Pepper for Christmas. I think she knew she was being funny, but she said it in all seriousness, and guess what she had under the tree on Christmas morning: Dr Pepper.

Bella is my little partner. She doesn't care to watch TV or really ever sit down; she likes to be busy. She's always by my side, "helping" me work. I call her my personal assistant, and you would be surprised at what she can do at ten years old (her age at the time of this writing). We've been making television shows since she was a little girl, and she always makes friends with the film crew. She keeps them laughing behind the scenes. Her most recent nickname is "Barbara," because she's a little Barbara Walters when meeting new people. She can carry on a conversation with any adult by asking questions about their lives. She'll find out how old you are, how long you've been married, how many kids you have, and where you work. She is interested in other people and other people are interested in her. If you meet her once, you will look forward to the next time. She's quick-witted and a fun kid to be around. It's been a joy to be her mom, and I'm so excited to see how God will use her talents and specific traits for His work. He's got big plans for her.

Rebecca came to our family a little late, but we are sure glad she did. She was sixteen when we greeted her at the airport with WELCOME TO AMERICA signs and excitement in our hearts. She didn't speak much English, but we loved her immediately. Bella took hold of her hand and wouldn't let go. Sadie talked her ear off (even though Rebecca didn't have any idea what she was saying), and the boys tried to win her over by wrestling with her and playing hide-and-seek. Rebecca, for her part, was scared to death, but she was a trouper. I can't imagine being sixteen years old, moving to a new country, and living with a family I've never met. She was equal parts brave and sweet—and she still is.

We laugh a lot in our family, and Rebecca fits right in. She's got an easy spirit, and she can laugh at herself, which is an important trait for a Robertson. She's incredibly talented and creative and goes for what she wants in life. Because she came to America in her junior year of school, she didn't have enough high school credits to actually get her diploma. She received a certificate of completion from the high school she attended and then had to get her GED to get into college. Despite all of this, she then went on to graduate from Louisiana State University in just four years with a degree in fashion design, right on schedule—something lots of Americans can't do!

Rebecca does have a mom in Taiwan, so I've always been careful to respect that. We are her American family, though, and if I ever make the mistake of saying I have only four kids, the rest of our children are quick to point out I have five. She is an awesome big sister and has become a beautiful, talented woman of God. We claim her as our own and are so thankful she claims us too!

MAMAW AND PAPAW HOWARD

When Willie was just a little boy, Miss Kay worked at Howard Brothers Discount Stores, one of my grandfather's companies. When she went to work there, I am sure neither she nor my papaw Howard, my dad's father, had any idea our lives would be forever intertwined. God's plan for my family and Willie's did not start with us. He has used the two families to bless each other as far back as two generations.

My papaw Howard was an exuberant man and a tireless entrepreneur. He had a strong faith in God and a sense of determination that would not take no for an answer. If he wanted to do something and believed in it, he went for it. He was not afraid to take a risk; some of those risks failed, but others took off in very big ways.

When Papaw Howard wasn't working, he had all kinds of fun hobbies, one of which was taking me fishing. We had many good times together baiting hooks and casting lines. He was a man of many talents who never stopped dreaming and creating. For example, he wrote songs, and my siblings and I often sang along with him while he played the piano. At other times, we followed him as he marched around his living room singing at the top of his lungs for "exercise." He was a wonderful host and often held get-togethers at his house, which everyone enjoyed. Every New Year's Eve, he had a party at his home, and we all rang in the New Year singing praises to God.

Of all my papaw's ventures, one of the most fun (for me at least) was a singing group he started. The "stars" were four sisters who were friends of our family. They sang country music and called themselves the Steffin Sisters. Papaw Howard wrote their songs, started promoting them, and even made a couple of music videos I got to be in! The Steffin Sisters went on a European tour when I was thirteen years old, and I went along as the babysitter. We traveled to Sweden, Denmark, Norway, Ireland, and England for six weeks one summer, going from one music festival to another, and I loved every minute of it.

In addition to being a great businessman and providing so much fun and entertainment, Papaw Howard gave me a strong legacy of faith. His commitment to Christ has outlived him; he is still helping lots of people through the ministries he helped start, such as the Christian camp Camp Ch-Yo-Ca, where my parents met and where I first laid eyes on that cute Willie Robertson when I was in third grade. He also played a huge role in founding the Christian school I attended, where all the Robertson children go today. He was instrumental in helping establish the many ministries our church still supports today, as well, including World Radio and Relief Ministries. In addition, he founded a Christian publishing company called Howard Publishing (now called Howard Books) and wrote many songs that churches all around the world still sing. He was a man who lived for God and did everything he could do to impact this world in positive ways. I think he did an amazing job!

Papaw's wife was my mamaw Howard. One of my favorite memories of her is that she often took me to a local nursing home and we passed out Little Debbie Nutty Bars to the residents. She had the sweetest, kindest spirit, and I cannot imagine her ever saying a bad word about anyone. She also had the gift of hospitality and invited someone from church over every Sunday for lunch.

Mamaw was also a prayer warrior. The Bible teaches us to "pray without ceasing" (1 Thessalonians 5:17, NKJV), and she did! She always seemed to be reading her Bible and often read verses to my cousins and me. She recited some of her favorite verses every night, and everyone who spent the night with her got the verses read over them in the beautiful old King James Version. One of her favorites was Isaiah 41:10: "Fear thou not; for I am with thee: be not dismayed; for I am thy God: I will strengthen thee; yea, I will help thee; yea, I will uphold thee with the right hand of my righteousness." I can still hear her sweet voice reading those words today and they still bring me comfort when I think of them.

Mamaw Howard often took me to a local nursing home and we passed out Little Debbie Nutty Bars to the residents. —*Korie*

Not long before I started writing this book, my mamaw passed away. At her funeral I heard stories I had never heard before about her helping people. I knew she had helped many, many people in many ways, but at her funeral I realized that her legacy of caring for people was even more powerful than I knew and went far beyond the stories I knew.

Mamaw Howard was a kind, sweet, lovely lady, but she was a strong woman too. She had a lot of struggles in her life, but she overcame them all. She always looked to God for help and strength and always praised Him in everything she did.

Papaw Howard was a good provider for Mamaw and their family. They were very well-off by the world's standards, but that was not important in either of their lives. Mamaw could have had any jewels, fancy cars, or anything else she wanted, but those things did not matter to her. Helping others and putting God first was what her heart was after. My papaw called her "Queenie." He loved and cherished her, and she did him, all the days of their lives.

MAMAW AND PAPAW SHACK

My mamaw Jo Shackelford, my mom's mom, is always stylish and beautiful but quick to point out that it's what's on the inside of a person that counts. One of her sayings is "Pretty is as pretty does." She is a living example of that generations-old truth.

Mamaw Jo can do anything. When my mom was growing up, Mamaw Jo sewed all of her clothes. She is quite a seamstress, and she cooks delicious meals, but her abilities go beyond her domestic skills. Now in her mideighties, she still owns and runs her own real estate business, as she has for years.

She and my grandfather, whom we called "Papaw Shack," lived in Shreveport when I was young, and I always enjoyed going to visit them. When I went, she made sure to have all of my favorite things. I love ice cream, and she made me homemade hot fudge sauce that was to die for.

I also remember her teaching me old-timey songs and playing "the Song Game," which I still play with my own kids. Here's how it goes: One person says a word and everyone else has to think of a song with that word in it. The first person unable to sing a song containing that word loses. Mamaw rarely loses at this game. She knows a lot of songs!

Mamaw Jo always made things fun and magical. She used to tell us she could make the traffic light change with magic. When we pulled up to a red light, she would recite this poem: "Rotten tomatoes and old tin cans, light on the corner of Main Street [or whatever street we were on], turn green, shazam!" And as soon as she said, "shazam!" the light would magically turn green!

Mamaw Jo has always been a strong lady. She's definitely not the kind of grandmother who will let you win at a game just because you are a kid; she wants you to earn the victory. She's a competitive Scrabble player, and when I was growing up, she and I played games all the time, everything from checkers to Old Maid. She beat me often! Now, carrying on the family tradition, Bella loves to go over to Mamaw Jo's house for late-night games of Uno, and they keep a running tally of who has won the most. She is so proud of each of her grandchildren and great-grandchildren and makes sure we all know it!

Mamaw's husband, Papaw Shack, always had a hug and a kind word for everyone. He passed away in 2008, and I still often meet people who tell me how much my papaw Shack meant to them. He worked hard all his life; his dad left his family when he was a young boy, and he worked as a janitor in his school when he was just in middle school. He said they were "so poor they couldn't pay attention." He loved his family and everything he did was for them.

My cousins and I know Papaw was our biggest supporter. He loved basketball. In fact, during World War II, he was on a team for the marines, a group that played exhibition games to boost the morale of the troops. That turned out to boost his morale, too, because he met my mamaw when he was a basketball player and she was a cheerleader. Papaw attended every one of his grandchildren's basketball games, but he also loved to hear about everything else we had going on. He wrote sweet notes to me, often encouraging me and telling me how proud he was of me. His family and his faith were his life.

Mamaw and Papaw Shack loved each other dearly. Anyone could tell each was the other's best friend. They worked together in their real estate business and enjoyed the simple blessings of life, such as waking up early, having coffee, and reading the paper together. When Mamaw Jo and Papaw Shack had people over for a meal, she was the cook, but Papaw always helped her with the dishes afterward. They were a great team, and I am thankful to have had that example of a husband and wife working together. It's something Willie and I have emulated, only he's the one doing the cooking, and I'm the one doing the dishes. I am so blessed to have had my papaw as my grandfather and to still have Mamaw Jo in my life today.

GRANNY AND PA ROBERTSON

I treasure who my grandparents were and who my mamaw Jo still is; I also appreciate having the chance to know Willie's grandparents, Granny and Pa. They lived close to Phil and Miss Kay for many years when Willie and I were dating, but they had to move away because their little house on the river suffered major flood damage. The house was old before the flood, and after the water got in it, it simply was not worth saving. Granny and Pa moved to Shreveport to live with Phil's sister, and except for holidays we did not see them nearly as much as we had in years past.

Granny really enjoyed making quilts, and not long after Willie and I married, she offered to make me one. This was during the time when the "country Americana" theme was popular and I found a design I wanted. It included red, blue, and black-and-white-checked fabric. She said the black-and-white check nearly caused her to go blind, but she made the quilt for us, along with a dust ruffle and pillows to go with it. I loved it and used it on our bed for the first couple of years of our married life.

Willie and I had a special visit from Granny the year Bella was born—on Granny's ninety-second birthday. Granny loved the thought of sharing a birthday with a great-grandchild, and she offered to come "help" with the new baby. Now, remember, she was ninety-two, so she wasn't much help, but I will cherish the memories of that time forever. She gave me advice on taking care of a newborn (even though I already had three babies) and helped as much as she could. We sat and talked and loved on little Bella those first few days of her life. Granny had made Sadie a quilt when she was born, and she crocheted a blanket for Bella.

Pa passed away not long after Willie and I married, so he did not ever know our children, but I will never forget his funeral. It was in the small country church he and Granny attended when Phil was young, and the congregation that day was full of bearded men! We sang a lot of old songs and hymns, and all the men sang at the tops of their lungs. Many kind words were said about Pa, and since the Robertsons can always laugh at themselves, even the funeral included funny stories. That day, I felt taken back in time to a different era, and I could sense the strength of the community that Granny and Pa enjoyed and the hard work it took for them to keep their family together.

Through it all, Granny and Pa stuck together, through good times and bad, for richer or poorer. When I attended Pa's funeral, I could sense the

When I attended Pa's funeral, I could sense the roots of the Robertson family and the foundation that made Phil who he is, which in turn made Willie the man he has become. —*Korie* roots of the Robertson family and the foundation that made Phil who he is, which in turn made Willie the man he has become. That's how generations work, so I believe those same good qualities—along with characteristics of the Howards and Shackelfords—are in my children too.

MY MOM AND DAD

Willie and I both have deep roots in Louisiana. Both sets of my grandparents have lived in the state for years, just as Granny and Pa did. Willie and I currently live on some property my grandfather once owned. Members of my extended family have lived close together, on the same street, for generations. Now my parents, Johnny and Chrys Howard, live right next door to Willie and me—and we did that on purpose! I love living so close to them, and I do not take that blessing for granted. My parents are always there for me, and with the busy lives and unusual schedules Willie and I have, that is so helpful. Besides Willie and me, they are our children's biggest cheerleaders, and they never—I mean *never*—miss an activity our kids are involved in. They are such an integral part of our children's lives, and all our kids know they can count on them or turn to them for help, no matter what they want or need.

The kids—mine and Willie's, those who belong to everyone else in the family, and even close friends—call my parents "Two-Mama" and "Two-Papa." There's a great story behind those names.

John Luke and Sadie are only twenty months apart in age. When I was twenty-six weeks pregnant with Sadie, I went into premature labor. The doctors were able to stop the labor but placed many restrictions on what I could do. The same thing happened again when I was about thirty-one weeks along, so I went on bed rest for about five weeks. At that time, John Luke was only a year and a half old and was busy, busy, busy. My mom had to help out a lot, and he loved being with her.

At only about eighteen months old, John Luke was not saying many words, but he could definitely say "Mama," so during this time he called both my mom and me "Mama." We tried to figure out another name for him to call Mom, but nothing stuck.

One day, after Sadie was born, I was driving with him in the car and he kept saying he wanted mama. I said, "Mama is right here," and he said, "No, Two-Mama." I realized he was asking for my mom. He has called her Two-Mama ever since, so we dubbed my dad Two-Papa. They are the best grandparents you can imagine. All of our kids, plus the other Robertson kids and many close friends of the family, love Two-Mama and Two-Papa.

God has really blessed me with an awesome family, not just with Willie and our kids, but throughout many generations. Our kids are not all old enough to fully understand and articulate the amazing legacy they have, but they definitely get it and appreciate it. I pray and believe they will carry on our family's faith, good qualities, and ability to make a difference for God for the rest of their lives.

20

GENERATIONAL BLESSINGS

Missy

When I think of generations, I think about the legacy and influence the people in each generation pass to the next one. Jase and I started dating when we were very young and had the opportunity to basically grow into adulthood together. Because of this, we have shared many "firsts" together. When our dating relationship started to become more serious, we made a commitment to stay sexually pure until our wedding night. Each of us had this goal before we started dating, but when we fell in love, that goal became one for each other as well. I knew that God expected this purity from His children, and I trusted God enough, even at my young age, to understand that His way was the best way. Jase and I reached our goal after dating two years, ten months, and two days. But who's counting? We were! Whew! We made it!

That night was the first sexual experience either of us had ever had, and we have only known each other since then. Being pure and faithful to each other and to God is a top priority for us to this day. Our decision to remain pure is something we

Our wedding night was the first sexual experience either of us had ever had, and we have only known each other since then. —*Missy*

have not been silent to our children about. The older we get and the older our children get, the more we realize how hard accomplishing that was and still is for kids today. We built our relationship on a spiritual foundation many years ago, and we feel a great responsibility to pass that spiritual foundation on to our children. At the time of this writing, our oldest child, Reed, is eighteen; Cole is sixteen; and Mia is ten.

PREPARING FOR A NEW GENERATION

When Jase and I married, we decided to wait a few years before having children. We wanted to spend this time together, just the two of us, before starting a family. We also wanted to prepare as best we could before starting to raise another human being. We felt like this was a huge responsibility. Once we began contemplating starting our family, I went to as many Christian parenting classes as I could find. We are blessed with many qualified and talented speakers in our church, and I was there every time the doors were open.

During one of those classes, a lady I still admire greatly said, "The best gift you can give your children is to love your husband." I first heard this when I was pregnant with Reed but have kept it close to my heart for the past eighteen years. I can honestly say my kids are confident in the fact that their mom and dad are completely committed to each other and to God, no matter what circumstance we face.

Since we have been in the limelight of *Duck Dynasty*, many women have approached Jase in person and on social media. However, because of his commitment to his Creator and to me, our family has become even stronger. Jase tells me almost every day how beautiful I am. He tells our teenage boys in front of me, "Your mama is one hot-lookin' woman!" They just laugh. No matter how difficult a situation may become, neither Jase nor I is going anywhere.

Our kids are also confident that their parents try to make decisions from a spiritual point of view. This doesn't mean we succeed every time, but our kids know, without a doubt, that we love God more than anything else in the world. When we fail, we have a Savior who forgives us and encourages us to try again. We try to do the same with our kids. When they fail, we are disappointed, but we try to show them that they are forgiven and encourage them to get back up and keep going. Living a spiritual life with God at the forefront is top priority for me, and passing that on to my children is my ultimate goal. I thank God for the previous generations who have influenced both Jase and me in this regard.

My Early Years

My parents moved to West Monroe when I was six months old. They grew up in New Mexico and Texas, so they were leaving all family behind when they made the move. They had no friends and knew no one; they simply moved on faith when my dad accepted a minister position at a church, the same church we still attend today. Because we did not live close to any family, I saw each set of my grandparents only once or twice a year. Because of this, I never formed a close bond with my grandparents. My dad was an only child, and his parents were not pleased with his decision to move away from them; this made their relationship very strained.

My mom was the oldest of five children, so she grew up in a very busy household. Each was expected to pull his or her weight. When my mom was fifteen years old, her baby sister, Bonny, was born. Five years later, my mom married my dad, and when she was twenty-three she had me. Since my aunt Bonny is only eight years older than I am (the same age difference between Reed and Mia), she became like my older sister.

Going to Grandma and Grandpa's house in Austin, Texas, meant I could see Aunt Bonny. For a while, we fought like cats and dogs. I was just far enough behind her in age to really bug her. I thought she was the coolest girl I ever knew. She grew to tolerate me over the years, and now we are very close. At the time of this writing she is working for Jase and me, assisting us with business affairs.

Since we traveled to Grandma and Grandpa's house mostly on holidays, that meant all the other aunts, uncles, and cousins would be there too. Their house was full of people for the entire week. It was so much fun! My mom's parents remind me so much of Phil and Miss Kay. Their house was always open to anyone who needed a place to stay. They supported missionaries who lived abroad and always helped students who were being trained in seminaries. They believed in God and have always been active in their church. I remember one Sunday—I think I was about twelve years old—when the entire family was together at their church; we got up onstage and sang the "Hallelujah Chorus"! Not many families can say that.

THAT ROBERTSON GENEROSITY

When Jase and I started dating, he introduced me to Granny and Pa. Not too long after we married, the flood forced them to move to Phil's sister's house about an hour away. Pa was getting feeble and sick and was soon moved to a nursing home. We didn't get to see them much after that.

Our daughter, Mia, was born with a cleft lip and palate that required multiple surgeries and procedures during the first few months after her birth (I'll tell her story in greater detail later in the book). On the way to her first surgery, we stopped to see Granny. Granny pulled Jase and me into her bedroom and offered to give us money for Mia's initial operation. Even though we didn't have nearly enough to cover our costs, we knew Granny sure didn't have it either. We hugged her and told her we were fine, that we didn't need anything. She made us promise that if we did need something, we would ask for her help. Of course we agreed. It was such a selfless act of generosity on her part, and I will never forget it.

Granny also made all of our children homemade afghans when they were born. Mia has had that blanket beside her through every surgical procedure. She's ten years old and still sleeps with what's left of it today.

A MUSICAL FAMILY

All of my aunts and uncles are musical, and my mom has a degree in music education. I was in Mom's choruses and special music projects until I graduated high school. I didn't know how good she was until I went to college and was in the performing choir. I've sung in several different groups and choruses throughout my life, but no director has ever compared to my mom. She is a perfectionist when it comes to music. She is never pleased with *good enough*. I have adopted that same mentality when it comes to music, and I work very hard at it.

Reed, Cole, and Mia all have a musical ear and have great singing abilities. Currently, Mia takes piano lessons. While I would have loved for the boys to take lessons when they were younger, our budget did not allow it. However, over the last few years, both Reed and Cole have taught themselves how to play the piano by ear and by watching how-to videos on the Internet. They have also taught themselves to play the guitar, ukulele, cajón drums, harmonica, and any other musical instrument they can get their hands on. We love singing together as a family and have started adding that to our family appearances. Actually, nothing gives me more joy than to stand side by side with my kids and sing praises to our God and Savior.

My mom is a big supporter of my kids' musical endeavors. She comes to all their performances and recitals and is happy to give advice, if they so desire. Music is and has always been a big part of my life. I'm glad my mom gets to share it with my kids and me.

SURROUNDED BY GENERATIONS

Unlike me, my kids have grown up with both sets of grandparents living in the same town where they live. What a blessing it has been! Over the years, the grandparents have been a great help to Jase and me. When we go out of town, somebody is at home to see to the kids, take them to school and pick them up, feed them, take them to practices and games, and take care of other things they need.

My dad calls me often and says, "Can I help you with the kids today?" He has an old Model A car he sometimes picks them up from school in. When the boys were little, they would call it the hot rod. Now that they are older, they don't think it's so cool. But they had many fun times in that car with my dad with the top down, going to Sonic and ordering ice cream and cheese sticks after school. He never let me eat ice cream in his car when I was a kid! My dad would spoil them rotten if I let him. Funny how grandparents do things for their grandkids that they would never do for their children. I guess Jase and I will experience that one day too.

Making the most of generational influence means grasping the good from those who came before you and doing your best to weed out the bad.

—Missy

One tradition my dad has with my kids is that every time they spend the night at my parents' house, usually on weekends, my dad takes them for doughnuts the next morning. If they keep them on a school night, he still takes them for doughnuts. Since school starts at seven forty-five A.M., this means they are at the doughnut shop before seven in the morning. But they love it! My dad shows my kids how special they are by spending time with them. He did the same for my brother and me. My parents are right beside Jase and me at every one of my kids' ball games, track meets, performances, recitals, and birthday parties. They wouldn't want to be anywhere else, and I am very grateful for their help, support, and unconditional love.

Making the most of generational influence means grasping the good from those who came before you and doing your best to weed out the bad. We all want to pass down the best to our children, and we all hope they forgive and forget what's not so good. That's a consistent trait throughout all generations. We want our kids to have it better than we did.

Part Five

SOMETIMES MIRACLES HIDE

And we know that God causes everything to work together for the good of those who love God and are called according to his purpose for them.

ROMANS 8:28, NLT

21

INTRODUCTION

Jessica

Bruce Carroll sang a song that was popular in the early 1990s, when I was just a preteen. But its message never grows old, and its title is simple: "Sometimes Miracles Hide." When we're in the midst of downright difficult circumstances, we can't always see that God is doing something great in our lives. Sometimes challenges and hard times can be so heartbreaking that all we can do is survive. But then, once we've survived, we see that God was working a miracle right in the middle of our hardships.

I have seen Missy and Jase walk this kind of journey since 2003, when their daughter, Mia, was born with special needs. Missy will write more about it in this section of the book, but I just want to say that they have been amazing as they have gone through situations not

> **When we're in the midst of downright difficult circumstances, we can't always see that God is doing something great in our lives.**
> **—*Jessica***

many parents have to go through. I remember being with Missy in the ultrasound room when she first wondered if there was something different about her baby. From that day until now, she and Jase have dealt with some unique challenges, but they have met them all with faith and trust in God. Now everyone in our family adores Mia, and we love having her in our lives.

I am also aware that Miss Kay suffered some very hard times with Alan and Jep as teenagers. As Jep's wife, I cannot even begin to thank his brothers and parents enough for the way they intervened in his life when he was in trouble. Sometimes I still get tears in my eyes when I think about how much Jep's brothers loved him when they first told Phil and Miss Kay he needed help. Had the brothers not cared enough about Jep to plan a family meeting to confront him—and had Phil and Kay not practiced tough love—I might not have the husband and family I have today. I will always be in awe of how much Jep's family loved him and grateful for the way they handled that situation.

Both Kay's situation and Missy's seemed overwhelming at times. Missy and Jase still face challenges. But both circumstances have proven to our family in up-close, personal ways that God can do miracles when it looks like nothing good can happen. When the world would refer to a situation as "bad," not only can God work it for good, He can do something miraculous.

22

TOUGH LOVE

Miss Kay

I love my boys! In the early days, the three oldest ones and I had to stick together just to survive. By the time Jep came along, Phil was an entirely different person than he was when Alan, Jase, and Willie were little. But in those early days, the oldest sons and I endured some lean, frightening, and difficult times.

Once Phil got his life straightened out by God's grace, I hoped my hardest days were behind me, and in many ways they were. But I did face two more situations that completely tore me up. In their teenage years, both Alan and Jep strayed from the way they were raised and did things they should not have done. These two boys reminded me of the Bible story about the Prodigal Son (Luke 15:11–32). They both went their own ways for about two years, and those experiences were very hard on our family. One thing that was very difficult for me was that they were both drinking, and I especially hated that because I had such bad memories of what alcohol had done to my mother and to Phil.

Today, I have a true passion to help people fight for their marriages whenever I can. I also come into contact with a lot of women whose children are far from their families and far from the Lord. Sometimes, when people only know me from *Duck Dynasty*, they think I have spent my whole life in the kitchen, happily feeding my tight-knit family. They do not think I could ever truly understand real pain, especially the depth of the pain of a broken marriage or a wayward child. I do. From years of personal experience with the pain, disappointment, and devastation, I really do understand.

I read the Bible a lot, and it has some great stories about miracles. One time, God completely dried up an entire sea so a whole nation of people could cross it on dry land and escape an army that was trying to kill them. We do not see many miracles like that one today, but I know God is still able to do them and that He does all kinds of other miracles every day. I have seen them, and I have even experienced them in my own life.

My loving, happy marriage with Phil is a miracle. *Duck Dynasty* is a miracle, not because our family has a television show, but because our family is *together*. Most people have no idea how close Phil and I came to breaking up years ago. We are only with each other right now because God did something miraculous in enabling us to forgive the pain of the past and to make a new start. The fact that all our boys are serving God today is also a miracle. Marriages can be healed, and prodigals can come home. I want everyone who is suffering in these kinds of situations to know that, and I hope this book will bring hope and encouragement to all who are going through what I went through years ago.

Amazing Little Boy, Amazing Man

Alan was a remarkable little boy. I truly do not know what I would have done without him during the years when Phil and I had so many problems. I did not live close to anyone in my biological family, and I was not involved in church during that time, so I had very little help or support. But when we ran into problems when Phil was drinking, Alan always stepped up to the plate. I did not have to ask him to help; he just did what needed to be done. As early as seven years old, he could feed and bathe babies almost as well as I could!

At a time when most boys his age were playing Little League baseball, Alan was taking care of his little brothers Willie and Jase. He did not get to do a lot of the fun things many children do; he helped me and definitely became my "main man." He was a much better caretaker for the younger boys than anyone I could have hired; he was totally trustworthy and dependable.

One time, Phil got more drunk than usual. It was scary, and I had to deal with a lot that night. In the middle of it all, Alan said to me, "It's okay, Momma. I fed the baby [Willie], and I burped him and changed his diaper. I fed Jason too. We're good. Don't worry about us."

Willie and Jase were so young at that time, they could not begin to understand everything Alan did and everything he sacrificed so they could stay alive and healthy. They will never know what all he did for them and for me. There were

Alan said to me, "It's okay, Momma. I fed the baby [Willie], and I burped him and changed his diaper. I fed Jason too. We're good. Don't worry about us."

—Miss Kay

times I did not think I could go on, but Alan made me feel like I could.

Alan always loved his family. One of my favorite stories about him is that as a teenager, he bought his own car. It was old, but it ran, and he paid for it with money he earned working at a grocery store and doing other odd jobs. He also helped Phil and me a lot at Duck Commander, but at that time we could not pay him anything.

Phil's truck broke down one day, and we could not afford to fix it. We really needed that vehicle and didn't know what to do. Without saying a word to us, Alan sold his car and gave Phil the money to get a new truck. Then Alan started over saving money to buy himself another car. That's the kind of thoughtful, generous person he is.

Alan was an amazing little boy, and he is an amazing man now, a man of strong character and integrity. He had more opportunities to be around my grandmother Nannie than the other boys, and he caught some of his heart from her. As I mentioned earlier, he also had a close relationship with a retired preacher, one of our neighbors in Arkansas, and I think that man had a powerful influence on him too.

Alan grew up to be a big help to Phil in the early days of Duck Commander and then to become a great preacher for many years. He still preaches from time to time, but now, he and his wife, Lisa, both work at Duck Commander. Sometimes, his work as a preacher makes people nervous. I am always sorry to hear about this, because he is the one who enabled the others in our family to be where they are today. Even though he has not been seen on *Duck Dynasty* as much as the other boys, our family would not be complete without him. Everyone loves and respects him so much, and he is a great blessing to all of us.

A SAD SURPRISE

In between being an amazing little boy and becoming an amazing man, Alan had some rough times. I was totally shocked when he began to change during his high school years. I will not write the whole story because it is Alan's to tell. Lisa has already shared some of it in this book, and Phil writes about it in greater detail in his book, *Happy, Happy, Happy.* I just want to say that I was surprised and heartbroken to find out about the choices Alan had made and the way he was living.

I only knew Alan was drinking because Jase told me. At first I thought there was no way it could be true—that Alan would never drink or get drunk because of everything he saw Phil go through. But it was true. One time when Alan and his friends got caught misbehaving, Phil told Alan he was disappointed in him and reminded Alan of what he (Phil) had put me through when Alan was young. I still remember hearing that lecture and Phil's saying at the end, "I hope you'll learn." Alan admits today that he did not learn.

Alan's behavior did not get any better. When he finished high school, Phil and I had to make a really hard decision. We told Alan he could not keep living in our house and do the things he was doing. We gave him a choice: he could straighten up, or he could go live with Phil's sister in New Orleans. He chose New Orleans! We hated to see him go but felt it was the best thing for our family as a whole. We did visit him a few times, but mostly we prayed for him.

Alan had a run-in with the police one Sunday morning while he was in New Orleans and as best he can recall, one of the officers said to him, "Let me talk to you. What are your mom and dad doing right now?"

"They're in church, where they always go," Alan answered.

"I knew," said the officer, "that you were raised different." In other words, the policeman could tell Alan was not what some people might call a "common criminal." The officer went on to speak some very strong words: "You have just done something really bad. Whatever you're doing here, pack it up. Go home and live like your mom and dad; go live like you were raised. I don't know your parents, but I have a feeling they will welcome you back like the Prodigal Son."

Phil and I had not been able to get through to Alan or influence him to change his ways while he was living with us, but that policeman in New Orleans sure got through to him. Sometimes we wonder if that policeman was an angel. Whether he was or was not, God definitely used him to get Alan back where he needed to be.

Alan left "the Big Easy" right away and came back to us. He started walking with God again; he reconnected with Lisa. He and Phil began studying the Bible together; Phil baptized him in the river by our house, and he has been a totally different person ever since.

It Happened Again

Jep only knows about the struggles his brothers, Phil, and I went through during our hard times because we have told him. Thankfully, he did not live through them. He only knows the new Phil, the man made new in Christ. Jep often says, "I'm glad I didn't know that old Phil. I like the one we have now!" Jep has always had a righteous, godly father who loves the Lord and loves the Scriptures.

Jep's experiences have been totally different from his brothers', but when he was old enough to make some important choices about his life, he went down a path very similar to the one Alan had taken years earlier. This situation, too, broke my heart, because until that time Jep had been nothing but a joy in my life. Phil and I had never had any major problems with him. Phil tells this story in his book, but it's important to me to tell it here from my perspective.

Phil and I were better off financially by the time Jep came along than we were when the other boys were young. We wanted Jep to have a biblically based education and to have the influence of going to chapel with his friends, so when he reached high school age, we sent him to a private Christian school, even though we struggled to pay for it. We hoped sending him to that school would mean he would have a good group of Christian boys as his friends and all of them would be good influences on one another.

For a while Jep did have a great group of friends and even a couple of nice Christian girlfriends. During his senior year, he got hurt playing sports and he went through a bad breakup with a girl. As a mom, I believe he started thinking his dreams were not going to come true, and he began hanging around with a new group of boys who were not good influences on him. I now know that when Jep went to visit one of those boys at home, some of the family was drinking and Jep drank with them.

After graduation, Jep moved into an apartment with his cousin. He did not live far from anyone in the family in terms of distance, but we did not see him as much as we had before. I knew Jep was not living as he had been raised, but I was not fully aware of all his struggles. I wrote him a lot of letters during that time, letting him know how much I loved him and how much God loved him.

THE CHOICE

My boys look out for one another. Jase is the one who told Phil and me when Alan had problems, and Willie is the one who let us know about Jep's bad behavior. Both Willie and Jase were typical boys and through the years they did the kinds of things boys do. But they did not get involved in the same activities Alan and Jep did, and when they saw their brothers in trouble, they were quick to run to their rescue and make sure they got help.

After Willie told us what was going on with Jep, the whole family decided to confront him about it. I don't think we called it an "intervention" back then, but that's the term that would be used today. We all got together at our house, and when Jep came over that night, he knew something was going on.

Basically, Phil said to him, "Son, this is what was reported to me." And he told Jep what he had heard. Jep could not deny it. His brothers were all standing nearby, and he knew they knew the truth.

They were not there to condemn him; they were there because they loved him so much.

Phil continued: "We don't support this. You can be on your own, and you'll be without my money and without a truck. Or you can live at home under house arrest. If you do that, you will have to live by my rules because we are not going to continue to do what we have been doing."

Jep hung his head and started confessing everything he had been involved in. Phil was crying; I was crying; Jep's brothers were crying. We all assured Jep that God would forgive him and we would too.

The next thing Jep said to Phil was heart wrenching: "Dad, why did it take you so long to rescue me?"

Phil spoke gently and humbly to him: "I'm sorry I waited so long. We just didn't want to believe what we were hearing."

After that, Jep told us he wanted house arrest. He wanted to clean up his life and live with us, according to the standards we set. When our family meeting was over that night, Alan, who was married by then, left our house and headed back to his home in West Monroe. He stopped along the way, got out of his car, went into a field, and fell to his knees weeping. He knew Jep could have died if his brothers had not told us what he was doing. He understood, in ways none of the rest of us ever could have, what it meant for us to reach out to Jep and call him to account for his actions. The Bible says God will go after one lost sheep and rejoice when that one is found, even

> The next thing Jep said to Phil was heart wrenching: "Dad, why did it take you so long to rescue me?"
>
> —*Miss Kay*

if there are ninety-nine others in the flock (Matthew 18:12–14). Alan understood, like no one else, what a powerful event had taken place in our home that day.

Eventually, after Jep had been home with Phil and me for a while, we allowed him to go live with a friend. We knew the friend's parents and they agreed to monitor his behavior. We saw Jep often during that time because he soon started studying the Bible with Phil and eventually brought his friends with him. One night he showed up at our house with fifteen people, wanting Phil to share the gospel with them.

Later, talking about his wild days, Jep told me, "Mom, I might have done all that stuff, but I always felt guilty about it. Your letters really meant a lot to me."

LOOKING BACK

As I think back now on those painful days years ago, I do not question the way Phil and I handled the situations with Alan and Jep. We used tough love with both of them, but because each of the boys is an individual, we could not handle both situations the same way. We felt we had to ask Alan to leave our home for a season, while we believed we could let Jep choose for himself whether to stay with us or to move out. Sometimes I wonder what would have happened if we had not done anything. What if we had not been willing to face the truth and confront our sons about it? Where would they be today? We cannot say. We are just thankful they did not continue on the paths down which they were headed.

No parent wants to go through situations like these, but plenty of parents do. And plenty of *good* parents do. All parents have to make their own decisions about how to deal with their children when these things happen. I would not presume to tell anyone what to do, but I do want everyone to know that just because a young person strays from his or her upbringing does not mean he or she is a lost cause. Sometimes, as in Jep's case, the love of family will bring people back to their senses and cause them to start replacing their bad choices with good ones. Sometimes, as happened with Alan, God will use a total stranger to help a person see the truth.

I like to say that all of us are imperfect people following a perfect Christ. That's just as true for people who get themselves in trouble as it is for those who don't. *All* of us have flaws and weaknesses. The point is that no matter what we do or how far we stray, we can always call on the perfect Christ to help us. In my own life, and in the lives of many other people, I have seen Him do this in the most amazing ways.

23

A MIRACLE NAMED MIA

Missy

**Behold, children are a heritage from the Lord, the
fruit of the womb is a reward.**

—PSALM 127:3, NKJV

Every child is a miracle. Jase and I have three of them, one of whom is our daughter, Mia. She is smart, strong, self-confident, happy, and a good friend to everyone she knows. On top of that, she has overcome a *lot* in her young life, and she is a continual reminder to all of our family that God will never leave us or forsake us. Deuteronomy 31:6 says, "Be strong and courageous. Do not be afraid or terrified because of them, for the Lord your God goes with you; he will never leave you nor forsake you."

IT'S A GIRL

Jase and I had two boys, Reed and Cole, when I got pregnant again. That became a terrible experience with a tubal pregnancy, and I went through a very scary and dramatic situation when the surgery to remove that pregnancy went wrong, and I ended up losing the entire tube in a second operation. That time in our lives was sad and difficult, to say the least.

Not long after I healed physically from my surgeries, we were overjoyed when we found out I was pregnant again. A phone call from the doctor a few weeks later gave us a harsh reality check when she told me there was a problem with my blood work. To make a complicated situation easy to understand: my blood type is A-negative, and because I did not receive a Rhogam shot after my tubal pregnancy, I would be at risk for another miscarriage if this baby's blood type were positive. Without Rhogam, my body would see the baby as a foreign object and try to dispose of it until it succeeded.

When I asked what the chances were for this baby to have a negative blood type and not be at risk, I was told that since Jase and I both have negative blood, 99 percent of all our pregnancies would result in a baby with positive blood, but there was always that 1 percent chance I could have a baby with negative blood. Both of my boys are positive and our lost baby had also been positive. The doctor told me our goal for this pregnancy was to make it to twenty-six weeks before taking the baby by cesarean section, because it would have a better chance of surviving outside my body than inside. This sobering news drove Jase and me to pray—a *lot,* much more than usual—about our baby.

There was no way to test the baby's blood in utero, so a specialist monitored my condition using markers in the blood work. If they began to go up, I would not be able to carry the baby to term. Miraculously, they did not! Because of that, we concluded that, statistically, our baby was one in one hundred. We have now confirmed that; that baby was our daughter, Mia, and she has negative blood.

With the crisis involving the blood type behind us, Jase and I quickly moved beyond the anxiety it had caused and regained our previous sense of joy about our new baby. Since we had every reason to believe the child was healthy, we could hardly wait to find out whether we were having a boy or a girl. We learned at twenty weeks that she would be a girl, and we were thrilled. We loved having two boys, but we wanted a girl in our family too.

TECHNOLOGY BECOMES A BLESSING

At that time, in 2003, four-dimensional ultrasounds were new, and people in the medical field were very pleased with the quality of the images they provided. So at thirty-one weeks, I scheduled that scan "just for fun," to see the new baby in a more detailed way. Jase had been present for my other ultrasound, but he was not with me that day. I did have several spectators, though, including Miss Kay, Lisa, Reed, Cole, and Jessica. We were all so excited!

Our excitement soon turned to concern when I asked the tech, "Does her nose look a little bit smushed?"

The look on her face told me she thought something was wrong.

"I need to get the doctor," she said as she turned to leave the room.

Miss Kay and Jessica took Reed and Cole out of the ultrasound room, and Lisa stayed with me. When the doctor saw the ultrasound, she confirmed what the tech had feared: the baby had a cleft lip. She could not tell how severe the problem was nor whether the palate was involved, but she did tell us clefts are often associated with a variety of other physical problems and syndromes. All she could say was, "We'll have to wait and see."

Miss Kay called Jase, and he came to the doctor's office so we could talk to the doctor together. While waiting on the doctor in the waiting room, Jase put his arm around me and said, "Well, we'll just have to teach her that beauty is on the inside." This is definitely *not* what I wanted to hear at the time. I wanted to hear that it was all a mistake, that we would get a second opinion, that this little girl we had waited on for so long was going to be born perfect. I didn't know this child yet, but I did know I already loved her. I also knew I didn't want her to suffer in any way, physically or emotionally, and I knew this condition would cause both.

> When the doctor saw the ultrasound, she confirmed what the tech had feared: the baby had a cleft lip. —*Missy*

Needless to say, our families rallied around us for encouragement and support, with a lot of tears. After a few days of grief and disbelief, I went into work mode. I learned all I could about this condition and started trying to find out where we could get her the best medical care. As hard as it was to find out my baby was going to be born with problems, I am very thankful for that 4-D ultrasound technology. Because we knew ahead of time, we had a chance to prepare ourselves and to arrange the care and services we would need for her. I cannot imagine how difficult it would have been had we been faced with trying to do all that and make major decisions for her in the moments and weeks right after delivery.

WE ONLY WANTED THE BEST

Knowledgeable people recommended two very good facilities to us, but both were teaching hospitals associated with medical schools. I decided I did not want my child to be a learning opportunity for some future doctor. I wanted the best, most experienced physician in the world. While we looked for that person, we prayed to the Great Physician and asked God to heal her in the womb.

The following Sunday morning, Jase and I shared our situation with our church family so they could pray for us. After the service, a couple approached us and said they had a client whose grandchild was born with a cleft palate. "Could we contact that family for you?" they asked.

"Yes!" we said, so relieved to think we might be able to speak with someone who could help us.

Later that night, I received a phone call from the mother of the child the couple had told us about. After we talked for a few minutes, she said confidently, "We have found the team to handle this problem." She went on to explain that their son was born with a cleft lip and palate six months earlier. They had researched surgeons who specialize in this area—and they located hundreds.

When her husband narrowed the search and began asking which physicians had been published, that field narrowed to only three—one in Los Angeles, one in Pennsylvania, and one in Dallas. They decided to contact the doctor in Dallas, Dr. Kenneth Salyer, the world-renowned craniofacial surgeon who separated a pair of conjoined twins in 2003. They were more than pleased with his team of doctors and were happy to share this information with us. We felt this was an answer to our prayers and that God had led us to this family, who ultimately became a large part of our support system.

At about thirty-four weeks, I communicated with Dr. Salyer's office and made arrangements for Mia to become his patient. They told us to call them when she was born, and they would see her one week later. Jase and I knew bringing this baby home would be a much different experience than we'd had with Reed and Cole, but we were comforted by the knowledge that Dr. Salyer was the right physician for us and the fact that plans were in place to see him so quickly after Mia's birth. So we did what all expectant parents do when the time of birth draws near: we waited for her to arrive.

SHE'S HERE!

I hoped to have a normal birth with Mia because when each of our boys was born, something was unusual. Reed was ten days late and faceup; he also got stuck in my pelvis during delivery. Cole decided to come three weeks early and was breech, requiring a C-section. I really wanted a nondramatic delivery with Mia!

Mia was due at the end of September, and I went to the doctor on September 11 for a normally scheduled appointment. My blood pressure was very high, so the doctor wanted to do a C-section right away. For various reasons—including the fact that my mom was out of town and I wanted her around for the birth—I asked if we could wait until the next day. The doctor agreed, as long as I promised to stay in bed and not move.

Jase and I headed to the hospital the next morning, and Mia was born later that day. As C-sections go, everything was fairly normal. Did God heal her in the womb? No. We know He could have, but He chose not to. All of the tissue from the top of her mouth to her nose was present; it just looked like someone had cut it with a pair of scissors because it was not fused together. We had wondered whether her palate would be affected or just her lip. Yes, we soon learned, the palate was cleft.

Mia weighed six pounds, nine ounces, so she was not unusually small. But she was born with a condition called wet lungs. Because of that and her cleft, the doctors sent her to the neonatal intensive care unit (NICU). When the specialists examined her there, they found that in spite of the wet lungs, her breathing was normal, and everything else they checked was fine. But once a baby goes into the NICU, that child cannot be released until he or she passes certain thresholds, one of which is volume of formula intake. She needed to be able to drink one ounce of formula in one sitting and keep it down before they would let her go. When she was born, she drank only a few milliliters at a time and had difficulty keeping it down. Getting to one ounce took her six days. We were so happy when she reached that point because we could take her home.

FIRST STEPS IN THE RIGHT DIRECTION

Dr. Salyer was not available as soon as we had hoped to see him because he was doing mission work overseas. Our first visit with him took place when Mia was seventeen days old. Of course, Jase and I both went on that trip to Dallas. My mom and dad, Miss Kay, and my aunt Bonny also went with us. We needed a lot of moral support! That first visit was grueling, and it literally lasted all day. Everything Dr. Salyer and his craniofacial team did had to be done, but much of it was uncomfortable for little Mia and all of it was stressful for Jase and me. By the time all the examinations were complete and all the test results were in, these experts were able to tell us with some confidence that, as far as they could tell at that point, Mia had none of the conditions that often accompany a cleft palate. They told us this was great news. We were so exhausted and so fried, we did not know what to think. We now know that it was indeed the best news we could have hoped for that day.

At that time, we thought Mia's condition could be "fixed." The doctors talked to us about a years-long schedule of surgeries. With so many procedures, we assumed, surely they could eventually make her mouth, palate, jaws, and other affected areas just like those of other children. That is not the case. Because Mia was born with her condition, the way her bones grow—or don't grow—impacts every-thing else. We have come to realize this condition cannot be "fixed" but will be managed for the rest of her life. We have been on a medi-cal journey with her since before she was born, and we will be on it for years to come.

SHE'S AMAZING

At the time of this writing, Mia is almost ten years old. She's an amazing little girl—confident, secure, well liked, and quite sassy and spunky. I could go on and on listing her good qualities. She is a leader among her girl cousins; whenever a group gets together, they want to know if Mia will be there. They love and support her, and she loves and supports them. Mia's brothers adore her and would take up for her in a split second if anyone ever gave her trouble, and she gets a kick out of hearing them say that to her.

Because of issues with Mia's bone structure and tissue, she is unable to form words the way most people do. But she taught herself to compensate for what she is missing physically and she speaks very clearly. She is not self-conscious; she interacts with others well and has fun wherever she goes.

People seem to love Mia. We have not had any serious experiences with people being unkind to her. One time, when Mia was about six years old, I heard a little girl ask, "What's wrong with your lip?"

Mia responded matter-of-factly, "I had surgery. You ever had surgery? It's really cool. I got ice cream." And that was the end of it. Her difference is not a deficiency, and that's because she knows how to handle it and she knows how to deal with other people. She does not let it stop her, slow her down, or keep her from doing anything.

> **Mia responded matter-of-factly, "I had surgery. You ever had surgery? It's really cool. I got ice cream." And that was the end of it.**
>
> —*Missy*

Mia has suffered a lot as she has undergone her surgeries, but she bounces back well from each one. At the time of this writing, she wears headgear. It's different from what most people think, as it does not wrap around the bottom of her face (like regular headgear for braces). It is specially designed to help align her top jaw with her bottom jaw, because the top one stopped growing due to scar tissue from a previous surgery.

She has to wear the headgear twelve to fourteen hours each day and was told she could not do any physical activity while she wore it. At first, the process of getting it off and on was difficult and painful since her mouth was so sore from the newness of all the attached metal. The doctor told her she did not have to wear it to school but would need to put it on as soon as she got home in order to get in all the hours. The reality of this additional life change for my child brought on a truckload of emotions for me. Since sleep only took care of nine and a half of the required number of hours, she and I both realized she still had at least three to four hours left each day. I was so sad to think she would have to give up riding her scooter, swimming, or jumping on the trampoline with Bella. However, Mia quickly figured out that if she wore the headgear at school, she could resume her normal playtime activities at home. This decision shocked all of her doctors and therapists. They told us that in all their years of practice, they had never had one patient wear it to school because of its visual effect.

Mia is a good patient, but she's an exceptional kid. We spend many hours sitting in waiting rooms with other families who are going through the same thing we are. We share stories and advice, and we marvel at how these kids cope with their conditions. Jase and I have seen firsthand that all of these kids are exceptional because of the suffering they endure. Romans 5:3–4 says, "But we also rejoice in our sufferings, because we know that suffering produces perseverance; perseverance, character; and character, hope." According to this scripture, character is not something we are born with; it is produced by persevering through suffering. I still pray that Mia will suffer as little as possible in this life, but at the same time I am grateful for what she has gone through. Without her suffering, she would not have the character she has today, the intense love and acceptance she has toward other people, and the enormous generosity that spills from her heart. Because of her character, she gives hope to other families going through similar hardships.

Jase and I are well aware that Mia will have many more challenges in the future. But with the character she has developed, with the faith we have as a family, with our trust that God will never leave us, we are confident she will not only handle them but overcome them and continue to amaze us all.

Part Six

LIFE IN THE LIMELIGHT

Let your light shine before others, that they may see your
good deeds and glorify your Father in heaven.

MATTHEW 5:16, NIV 2011

24

INTRODUCTION

A Message from the Wives

We are biased, of course, but we honestly believe we have the greatest fans in the entire world. We love them, appreciate them, and try to interact with them as much as possible. Having fans is one of many things we never dreamed would happen to us before *Duck Dynasty* went on television and became a hit. The visibility the show has brought to our family has changed our lives in some ways but not in others. For example, the show has given us lots of exposure, and some people say it has made us famous, but it has not changed who we are as human beings. It's relieved some financial pressure, but it has not changed our value system. It's put our family in the spotlight in ways that can be intense, but it has not affected the love and support we have for one another. It has definitely brought us closer together and hopefully it has brought love, laughter, faith, family, and ducks to millions of people around the world.

Korie: WE'RE ALL IN THIS TOGETHER

I think one of the best things about the increased visibility *Duck Dynasty* has brought to our lives is that we all experience it together. We feel blessed to be able to do the show as a family. It's not like one person suddenly has the attention of the world while the rest of us sit in the shadows. We have heard about families in which one person becomes famous, and it changes their family dynamic completely. The whole family moves to Hollywood and that does not always go well; sometimes the struggles and problems that result are almost insurmountable. When everything centers around one person, it can disrupt the family life.

In our family, we are all in the spotlight together. Fame has happened to all of us at the same time, and that keeps us normal and grounded. As my sister-in-law Jessica says, "We don't let anyone get too big for their britches." We see the fame and celebrity for what it is. We appreciate it, but we are not impressed with ourselves because of it. We are able to share both the burdens and the blessings of this unexpected and amazing opportunity, and that helps all of us deal with it better than any of us would on his or her own.

> I think one of the best things about the increased visibility *Duck Dynasty* has brought to our lives is that we all experience it together. —*Korie*

25

LIVING IN A GLASS HOUSE

Lisa

Alan and I did not appear on *Duck Dynasty* until season four, so we have not dealt with the spotlight in the same way others in our family have. We learned about it in an entirely different way that was sometimes just as intense. We were in the ministry for many years, and I found out soon after we started that a minister and his wife live in a glass house. Somehow, it seems that everyone sees, hears, and knows everything that goes on in your life! We quickly learned that we needed to be totally transparent. Now our lives are open books. If people need to know something about us, we want them to hear it from us in the most straightforward way, not through the grapevine after it has been embellished or misinterpreted.

We also want people to know it was God's power that helped us deal with all the difficulties we have faced through the years. Typically the church is a place where people find hope and healing, but in any church, there are some people who want to know all the "juicy stuff" about the minister and his family. This goes on everywhere. We are all human beings; some of us want to find the positive attributes of a ministry family, and others, unfortunately, want to find out the flaws and less-than-desirable qualities of church leaders. During our years in ministry, Alan and I learned to speak openly about our flaws and to accentuate what God has accomplished through us in spite of them.

I think one of the saddest things about living in a glass house, especially in the ministry, is that the children of the minister suffer so much during their growing-up years. Some people think the minister's sons or daughters should be perfect. These people do not take into account that they are children, and they will make mistakes—as all children do. There is no "special potion" we as ministers get to rub on our kids to make them act a certain way! We rub Jesus all over them with our love, devotion, and acceptance of them, but they still make mistakes, just like their minister parents! Okay, enough preaching. I think I might have started meddling. Whether a family lives in the spotlight because of a ministry position, a television show, or some other reason that brings visibility, there are special challenges that come with the increased visibility.

GOD PREPARES PEOPLE

When Alan and I look back on our years in ministry, we have a lot to be thankful for. We worked with a truly great church, we had some exciting opportunities to travel and do mission work overseas, and we served God alongside some incredibly faithful and really good people. We were always aware of those things. But we were not aware at the time that God had something else in store for us and that He was not only using our time in the ministry to help people in the present but He was also using it to prepare and train us for our future. Without the experiences we had and the lessons we learned back then, we would not have been prepared for the life we have today.

We often hear about people, especially young people, who are desperate to become "famous." We see people who think everything in their lives would be wonderful if they could just make it big and become a star. Many of them do not realize there is a price for fame and that there are both positive and negative aspects to living in the public eye. Without a well-grounded life and a strong support system, being a star has the potential to devastate individuals and their families.

We believe God prepared everyone in our family in different ways for the visibility we now have. For Alan and me, living in the glass house of ministry gave us a very firm foundation for the lime-light of the entertainment world. God always knows what's ahead for all of us. In His love for us and His desire for us to be blessed, He prepares us. When Alan and I worked at the church, we never dreamed we would someday be so involved in a TV show. God trained us in the relative safety of a church setting for everything we would deal with in the realm of television. He let us grow and make mistakes in front of a small, loving audience before He put our family in front of the whole world. We are very thankful He gave us the training we needed over a period of time, among family and friends, instead of just letting us wake up one morning with our last name as a household word.

I always want to tell people who have big dreams that we just never know what's ahead. We have to embrace every season God takes us through, trusting that He will use each one for our good and for His glory. We have to believe that if He wants to put us in the spotlight, He will prepare us for it and do it in such a way that we can handle it well.

I cannot imagine what *Duck Dynasty* would have done to our family had we not been ready for all the changes it brought and had we not been grounded in our faith and our family. A lot of people crave overnight success, but we are glad that did not happen to us. We see the wisdom and love of God in our lives as He spent years with us behind the scenes making us ready for the high level of exposure our family has today.

THE BEARDLESS BROTHER

One thing that sets Alan apart from the Robertson men who frequently appear on *Duck Dynasty* is that he does not have a beard. In fact, when the media heard he would appear on the show starting in season four, lots of headlines and articles identified him as "the one without the beard."

By the time a large audience began to hear about Alan and about the two of us as part of the Robertson family, we were well established in knowing that very little matters in life except pleasing God, pleasing each other as husband and wife, and honoring our family. We had learned the hard way that we could not please everyone around us, so we do not spend much

> **Our family members make plenty of mistakes, but we recognize them, own them, and make our apologies.** —*Lisa*

energy trying. We do our best to live our lives with integrity and to love and serve the people around us. We make plenty of mistakes, but we recognize them, own them, and make our apologies. None of us has any room in his or her life to judge the others. Rather, we work to love and forgive each other. Our family has hearts that seek after God; I can say that with total confidence about each and every person in our family, and we all do the best we can to fulfill our responsibilities and enjoy the life God has given us.

WE WANT TO BE GOOD EXAMPLES

Because of the publicity our family receives, we are responsible for holding our standards high. We want to be good examples. That starts at home long before it shows up in front of the camera. Though I do not often appear on *Duck Dynasty*, I do participate in plenty of casual conversations about the show with my sisters-in-law and Miss Kay. We talk about the fact that the impact of everything they do is magnified because they are in the limelight. The way they dress, the way they talk to their husbands and children, the way their children talk to them, the way they control their actions, and all kinds of other things make statements about who they are. Alan's and my children are grown, but we have grandchildren who have to learn these lessons too. We must teach each generation about these truths. Once a show is filmed and goes on the air, they do not get a do-over and they do not get to go back and tell the world what they really meant. An audience takes things at face value and draws their own conclusions, which means first impressions are extremely important.

First impressions are just that—first impressions. You only get to make that first impression one time. If a person gets to know you and interact with you, a bad first impression can be changed. But with television, people do not get to interact with us and see us at our best. Our best has to be what we put in front of the camera every time it's on. We hope and pray our family is making an excellent impression on the world through *Duck Dynasty*, giving people a lot of good laughs. But even more important than the laughs, we want to be true to the fact that we love God, we love each other, and we desire—through the show—to honor Him, to honor one another, and to affirm the goodness of faith, family, and the true love of Jesus.

26

IT'S NOT JUST FOR US

Missy

As Jessica mentioned earlier in the book, I also have to laugh when I hear people talk about Korie, Jessica, and me as gold diggers. I think, *Oh please! Jase was skinning raccoons for extra money when Cole (our second child) was born!* The only gold I was interested in was Jason's old gold-colored Chevy, because it had a bench seat and I could snuggle up to him while he drove.

When *Duck Dynasty* started, we lived paycheck to paycheck. Most of us in the family did not really have anything extra. Jason and I often heard our friends talking about financial planning for their children's college careers, but that seemed almost impossible to us; we simply hoped our car kept running.

I will never forget the days, not so long ago, when instead of traveling around making live appearances for large audiences on weekends, Jason traveled to small towns to preach in churches and typically brought home some kind of honorarium that provided us with a little extra money. Financially speaking, we did not have much, but we were happy, and we had a good life. We were blessed before we ever dreamed of being on television. Now we are overwhelmingly blessed. We were blessed to have enough for many years; now we have been blessed with abundance.

GENEROSITY COMES FROM THE HEART

I have never been affluent; Jase hasn't either. Spending a lot of money on ourselves and "building barns and bigger barns" is not in our personalities. We have always tried to be generous, and *Duck Dynasty* has not changed that. Now we simply have a little more to be generous with.

I once heard a saying that went something like "If you won't share a peanut butter and jelly sandwich when you are poor, you won't share a steak when you are rich." Generosity comes from the heart, not from your bank account. In 1997, Jase and I built a house in the country. For six years before that, we had lived in a 1,099-square-foot two-bedroom, one-bath house in the middle of town. That was where we brought home our first child, Reed, in 1995. For six years, we hosted Sunday-night church fellowships in our house with anywhere from fifty to eighty people in our carport turned living room. Finally Jase said, "I just can't live here anymore. I really need to move to the country."

At that time, Duck Commander was still being run out of Phil and Miss Kay's house, and Jase was Phil's only help when it came to making duck calls. Since Phil and Miss Kay lived so far from town, we decided to try to move closer to them. Phil's good friend Mac had three acres next to his house and offered it to us for a great price. We built a four-bedroom, two-bath house on that property, where we lived for ten years and brought two more babies home from the hospital.

Since we were on a tight budget, our contractor offered many different ways for us to save money. He said, "Every corner we build is an added expense." So I said, "Then I want only four corners."

We made our front bedroom into a playroom with a glass-pane door in order to accommodate the many church groups and Bible studies we planned to have in our home. This way, kids could use that room quietly while the adults watched them during our Bible studies. It worked wondrously, and people could come to the gatherings without having to hire a babysitter.

I learned from watching Phil and Miss Kay what it means to use all of your resources in ways that help others. Jase and I understand that the material blessings we have are gifts from God, not something we earned ourselves. If you think you deserve something or have something because of your own deeds, it will be far more difficult to share it. Living a life of gratefulness and generosity is far more rewarding than counting your silver coins every night.

Now God has blessed us with a platform. The visibility and resources we now have were given to us directly by Him, and we know God has given them to us for a reason. That reason, I believe, is not to please ourselves; it's to help others. We have a beautiful home and nice vehicles, which we enjoy immensely. But they are only things. They are not nearly as important to us as people and our relationships with them.

WE RECOGNIZE OUR RESPONSIBILITIES

People who watch *Duck Dynasty* do not always realize that we have a family business—not just for television but in real life. We work hard, just like lots of other people in America. For some reason, God has seen fit to use us in the world of entertainment, and we believe He has a purpose and a plan in doing so.

All of us feel that the opportunities and resources we have been given are big responsibilities for the Robertson family as a whole and for each of us individually. This is something God has given us that does not ordinarily happen to many other families, and we want to be good faithful stewards of it. Jase and I talk to our children a lot about the parable of the talents. In Matthew 25:14–30, Jesus told a parable about a man who left on a long journey. Before he left he gave to one servant five talents (a type of money in New Testament times), to another two, and to another one. The one with five talents put his money to work and gained five more. The person with two talents also doubled his money. But the servant to whom he gave one talent buried it. When the man returned, he was very proud of the first two servants but very disappointed in the last one. Because the third servant had not used the talent he'd been given—but had buried it—he took that servant's only talent away from him. In other words, God gives what He feels we are responsible enough to use, and if we aren't responsible with it, He will take it away. In our family, we

> **We will make mistakes, misjudgments, and downright selfish decisions sometimes. But thanks to Jesus, we are given many more chances to get things right the next time.**
>
> —*Missy*

want to use what He gives us in all the right ways and never misuse it or fail to appreciate it. Will we always make the right decision? Sadly, no. We will make mistakes, misjudgments, and downright selfish decisions sometimes. But thanks to Jesus, we are given many more chances to get things right the next time.

JUST REGULAR FOLKS

Jase and I are very thankful to have our children in a school where teachers, coaches, and classmates treat them the same way they treat everyone else. They definitely don't get the star treatment, and that's the way we want it. Our boys have to work just as hard as their peers to make a sports team, and they will get benched as quickly as anyone else if they do not play well. I love that they do not get treated any differently from their fellow students.

My parents, along with four other couples, founded Ouachita Christian School in 1974, so in a way it feels like home to me. Korie, Jep, and I all went to school there, and Phil taught there for a while before he started Duck Commander. Now all the Robertson cousins go there. It's a school founded on Christian principles, and Jase and I know it is a place that affirms the values we have for our family. Everyone there treats us as though we are regular moms and dads— which, of course, we are—so we appreciate that. We can attend Reed's home football games and sit right there in the stands with the other fans and families, and no one bothers us. Even on the road at away games, our friends help keep us as anonymous as possible so we can enjoy being just parents. Sometimes it works; sometimes it doesn't. We try to accommodate as many autograph and picture requests as possible before and after those games and during halftime. But when Reed steps onto the field, we are there in full support of him and his teammates, and autographs have to wait.

OUR SACRED SPACE

One thing that really surprised me, and probably our whole family, after our show started was that people we did not even know came to our church to try to see us or to ask for autographs. I have sung on our church's praise team almost every Sunday for more than twenty-two years, and I love doing it. One Sunday after a very prayerful song, someone yelled from the audience, "Go, Missy!" I turned three shades of red, I'm sure. As our praise leader went right into the next song, a couple of men made their way over to where that person was sitting in order to defuse any potential problems. Nothing else happened, but obviously, the somber moment was lost, and the mood became very awkward and a bit tense.

We appreciate the interest in our family, but being able to attend services without distractions is important to us. We go to church to worship God and for fellowship with our longtime friends—people who knew us and loved us before our faces were ever seen on TV. We hope everyone who visits our church is blessed by being there, and we really appreciate all the people who respect us and respect our church family by allowing us to attend church uninterrupted.

We know this is only a season in our lives. It will not always be like this. One day, maybe sooner than we think, we will go back to being regular church members in a regular church on a regular Sunday morning. We might even miss being asked to take a picture during "meet and greet." Well, maybe "miss" is too strong of a word. Our church family is very special. Our services are incredible and our a cappella singing is inspiringly beautiful. People are completely uplifted when they visit our congregation, and it honestly has nothing to do with us. We are no more important than anyone else there. Every member makes it special. That's what is so great about God's family. Every part has a purpose—television star or not.

27

WE'VE COME A LONG WAY, BABY!

Miss Kay

After the way I grew up and all the hard times Phil and I have been through, who would have ever dreamed I would write about what it's like to live in the limelight? Back in the days when I lived in a trailer with three little boys, barely able to keep the lights on, who would have imagined I would ever be talking about being famous? Who would have thought I would have trouble finding a parking space at the Duck Commander office because so many fans had come to see it? Not me!

I appreciate everything *Duck Dynasty* has enabled us to do, but I have to say, there are both good and bad parts to it. Some things in our lives have gotten easier because of it, but others have gotten harder. For example, I love the fact that some of my grandchildren have opportunities to speak and can share their faith with large audiences. Also, I'm so glad my children are able to pay for their homes—that makes me really proud. But I am sorry for the freedom I have lost in my schedule and the freedom I have lost to be an ordinary, unknown person who just loves to cook and enjoy her family. I don't get to do family dinners the way I want to anymore. They have become much more structured, and a lot of times, we do them with a full television crew in my kitchen!

SO MANY VISITORS

I remember the carefree days when I could open my door on a beautiful morning and go outside in my pajamas without anyone seeing me. That almost never happens anymore, and I miss those times! Oh, I still go outside in my pajamas, but there's often someone standing nearby ready to snap my photo the second I go out the door. I have to pay a lot more attention to the way I look than I used to. I have to do my hair and my makeup, and I have to wear decent clothes, because every time I walk out, there's a good chance I will have my picture taken many times before I get back home.

I was raised on the Golden Rule: "So in everything, do to others what you would have them do to you" (Matthew 7:12). I do my best to live by those words, so when I get ready to say or do something that involves others, I try to ask myself if I would want them to do to me what I am about to do. I just wonder if the people who stand in my front yard with cameras flashing would want me standing in their yards taking pictures of them in their pajamas. Maybe only if I had a plate of hot biscuits to share!

I have to draw a line when I go out with my grandchildren to do something special. I have to tell people nicely that I cannot stop for a photo right then. Again, if they were out trying to have a special day with their grandchildren, I do not think they would want strangers trying to take pictures.

WE NEVER DREAMED . . .

When Phil and I moved to the river many years ago, we never in our wildest dreams thought we would have to put up a fence or a gate just to maintain a little privacy. We live so far out of town that we were totally shocked when people first started coming to our house trying to catch a glimpse of us. They came early in the morning, sometimes before I was even out of bed, and they came as late as eleven or twelve o'clock at night. Some of them even knocked on our door!

We eventually had to get a fence and a gate; this really went against our nature, because we have always wanted our home to be a warm and welcoming place for all our friends and family. We love to have people over, but when people we'd never even met started inviting themselves and showing up at all hours, we had to do something in order to maintain the privacy we have left. I need my home to be a safe haven, just like most other women do. And, like most people, I want to live in a place where my grandchildren and my family can be safe. I don't think that's too much to ask.

If we ever forget, in the midst of the fame, where we have come from, then I pray God will take it all away from us and move us right back to where we were in the beginning. I really do. I think a lot of us in the family feel that way. We do not want everything the show has done for us to change us in a bad way. Occasionally, Alan gets us together for a reality check. He talks to us about our lives, about how we are doing, and about not allowing our "stardom" to affect us negatively.

I am thankful for the great opportunities we have been given because of the show. Sometimes we get to stay in really nice hotels and when that happens, I try as hard as I can to be friendly and to talk enthusiastically to everyone. I do not care if a person is a housekeeper, a

> **If we ever forget, in the midst of the fame, where we have come from, then I pray God will take it all away from us. I really do.**
> —*Miss Kay*

maintenance worker, a concierge, or the owner of the whole hotel; I want to give everyone the same kind of attention and kindness. Everywhere we go, we see people who are working hard. I know what many of them are going through. I have not forgotten what it's like to struggle to make a living—and I pray I never do forget.

DON'T MAKE MOMMA MAD

There are only a few things in life that make me really, really angry. One of them is when people struggle in their marriages and refuse to fight for them, but I have already mentioned that. Another thing that infuriates me—and embarrasses me so much for the people who do it—is when women nearly fall all over my sons flirting with them. They try some of the most disgraceful things to catch Willie's, Jase's, or Jep's attention. Some of the behavior I have seen toward my sons—and even toward Phil and Si—is just shameful! I don't understand how people can let themselves act that way, and as a woman, I really am humiliated when other women do such things.

I realize all the boys are good-looking, and I know what great men they are, but *they're taken*. A lot of people don't respect the vows and commitments of marriage anymore and simply do not have any self-respect. They do not seem to have any reservation at all about flirting with men they know to be married. When people don't honor the fact that each of my sons already has the woman he has chosen, I want to say, "Come on! These boys are happily married men. Go find your own duck hunter!"

This kind of thing did not happen before we went on television, and I hate to see it happening now. As much as I enjoy interacting with our fans and hearing stories about the positive impact *Duck Dynasty* has had on so many people, I will never be okay with women chasing after my sons.

A GREAT WAY TO SHARE OUR FAITH

Though I don't like the flirtatiousness the boys have to deal with at times, I am grateful that the show gives us a way to share our faith and our values with millions of people. All that really happened to us is that some people at a television network saw something in us, liked us, thought we were funny, and realized we could make money for them. The entertainment industry is a very secular environment, but when we had a chance to get involved in it, we did and used it to share our faith.

I think about Phil's journey to faith in Christ. For many years, his journey through life was painful for him, for me, and for the boys. We prayed and prayed for him, and when he repented and got baptized, we were so happy we could hardly stand it. That man had a 100 percent turnaround in his life. And now, he tells everyone about it. He is the most courageous Christian I have ever known. He will share his faith with absolutely anyone. I am so glad God has given him—and all of us—a chance to do that in such a big way. The inconveniences and the sacrifices we make in order to have this opportunity are worth it.

28

WE'RE HAPPY NO MATTER WHAT

Jessica

I appreciate the fact that *Duck Dynasty* gives our entire family a chance to show the world who we are. When people ask me what makes us Robertsons the kind of family we are or what we do in order to have the kind of family life we enjoy, I have two words: "Robertsons love." That's the bottom line. To me, the best thing about the limelight and the exposure we have is that we get to present to the world the love we have for God and the love we have for one another. We also get to do a lot of good, whether that means calling attention to a good cause, donating money to charity (we have done events and given all the proceeds to charity), or just taking the opportunity to share love and kindness with the world. We have not always had those opportunities, and we are blessed to have them now.

When I think about what it means to enjoy some celebrity status and about how *Duck Dynasty* has changed our lives, I also have to think about how it has not changed us. For one thing, we are still the same happy, loving people we have always been. Jep and I have always found our joy in God and in our family. We have never been impressed by fame or fortune, and we still aren't.

By the time Jep came into the Robertson family, some of Phil and Miss Kay's major financial challenges were behind them. While Alan, Jase, and Willie remember times when their family struggled to buy groceries, Jep remembers that Miss Kay bought him a new G.I. Joe almost every time one came out. My upbringing was similar. Our family always had enough, and we took care of our belongings. I remember, as a fifth or sixth grader, when my parents bought us a trampoline. I thought we were *rich*. For all I knew, it might as well have been a yacht! I share those stories to make the point that Jep and I have always felt taken care of; we did not feel we lacked anything we needed. Now we want our children to feel the same way—whether or not we are on television, whether we have $500 in our checking account or $50,000.

TEACHING OUR CHILDREN

Children today face temptations that Jep and I never encountered. Technology alone has totally changed the way many children think about money and possessions. While I grew up having to save my money for something like a new bicycle and knowing I would not get another one for several more years, a lot of children we know have the latest electronics handed to them and then get new ones as soon as updates are available. We try hard to help our children understand what it means to earn their own money and make their own purchases and to appreciate and take care of what they have. We want them to realize they do not need the latest, greatest gadget. I did not even have a cell phone until I met Jep. I use my phone and laptop for many purposes, but I have no need to upgrade them every time I turn around.

I could hardly believe my ears the day one of our children told me we needed more square footage in our home. I didn't know she had ever even heard of square footage! Apparently, someone at school had been talking about moving into a larger house, and our daughter thought we should do the same. I said to her, "You know what? I am glad that family can have a bigger home, but square footage or having the biggest and best of anything does not make anyone happy. I'm happy. All my children are healthy; we have a nice home and food on our table. All our needs are met. We have a peaceful, happy life. We don't fight. And we're all together. If we get a bigger house someday, that would be great. But if we don't, I will still be the same happy person I am right here in this house. Having my dream house, a new car, or the nicest clothes will not make or break my happiness." I think she got the message!

It's more important for us to raise our children knowing Jesus Christ than it is to be wealthy from the world's perspective.

—Jessica

Joy does not come from what we have; it comes from knowing God. And God has blessed our family with so many gifts no amount of money could ever buy. I was content when Jep and I hardly had anything at all, and I am just as content now. We can truly say we are rich in love, and that is what matters most to us. It's more important for us to raise our children knowing Jesus Christ than it is to be wealthy from the world's perspective.

KEEPING OUR BALANCE

Jep and I are determined to stay happy and balanced, no matter what happens in our lives. Like everyone involved in *Duck Dynasty*, we had to make major adjustments to our schedule when it started. We suddenly had to squeeze filming, travel, speaking engagements, and other live appearances into an already busy life with four young children. The filming alone takes much longer than most people think. Even filming the short dinner scenes at the end of most of the episodes often takes one and a half to two hours. We have to add to that the time it takes for hair and makeup, which we do every time we film anything. And sometimes, the dinner scene is not filmed at a normal mealtime, so that throws off our schedules a little, but at least we can enjoy time with our family and have a good meal.

When *Duck Dynasty* started, Jep and I learned quickly we would have to monitor our lives closely and set firm boundaries in order to keep time from getting away from us and to keep ourselves from getting worn down. It did not take long for us to see how fast the scales of our lives could tip out of balance, causing us to feel burned out and empty. For me, especially, the travel can be grueling. Sometimes, when I'm on the road, I can get so tired and miss my kids so much that I want to cry. Every so often our priorities get out of balance, and we have to stop and get everything back in order. The great thing is that Jep and I are on the same page, whether the issue is raising the kids or our views on life in general. When I overextend myself, he can see it and he will let me know. I do the same for him, because we love each other and are on the same team; we are helpmates to each other.

Prayer is a big part of our lives, and Jep and I pray regularly about our commitments and our schedules. Is it important to be paid for a television show so we can have nice things? It's not nearly as important as providing our children with happy childhoods and not being so exhausted that we won't remember this time in our lives ten or twenty years from now. God blessed Jep and me with four sweet children, and it is our responsibility to teach them how to grow to be godly people, to make the right choices in life, and to treat others well. We continually ask ourselves what is most important in our lives. We realize our children are the youngest of the Robertson grandchildren, which means they might possibly spend more of their lives in the spotlight, starting at younger ages, than their cousins. We do not want them, or ourselves, to lose anything that is truly valuable in life just because we are on TV.

MAKING WISE CHOICES

One thing we have had to be very diligent about is teaching our children to choose their friends wisely. Our children have experienced a few instances in which others have been nice to them because of their last name. One of our daughters, Lily, is very shy when she is not around family. She did not have many friends during her first few years in school, but when *Duck Dynasty* started, she suddenly got a flood of invitations to do things with other children. We cannot judge anyone's intentions, but we did notice the dramatic increase in people who wanted to be her friend. We wanted to make sure the people who reached out to her were truly interested in *her*, not in anything else.

In helping our children choose good friends, we have taught them to pay attention to the way people treat others as much as they pay attention to the way people treat them. We have encouraged them to see whether the children who want to be their friends treat their teachers with respect and whether they are nice and kind to everyone. We have taught them to notice whether other children obey their parents, teachers, and others in authority. These are important values to us, and we want our children to choose friends who share them.

We have laughed at times because once *Duck Dynasty* went on the air, little boys started liking our daughter Merritt—who is nine years old at the time of this writing. She is a cute little girl, so I can understand this, but it could also be that they just want to meet Jep. Either way, it's cute! We might be a little concerned if she were really into boys, but she's not into them right now, thank the Lord!

We felt good about our youngest daughter, Priscilla, one day when we heard that Willie asked her, teasingly, "Do you want to be a TV star when you grow up?" She looked at him and answered humbly but matter-of-factly, "I already *am* a TV star." It was almost as if she were thinking, *Been there, done that. What's next?* At this point, she is unfazed by the whole television situation. It's part of her life, but it's not her whole life.

Our son, River, is the youngest member of the family and was only two years old when we started filming *Duck Dynasty*. He may get a few things other little boys do not have, and he will likely have some opportunities others may not, but Jep and I do not want him to have anything handed to him. We want him to know what it means to work hard and save and wait for what he wants. Our job as parents is to teach him those lessons.

GENERATIONAL LESSONS

When Jep was very young, his parents taught him the same kinds of lessons we want our children to learn. He tells a story about a time when he was a little boy and went with Miss Kay to take food to someone who lived in an underprivileged neighborhood. The person could not afford a very nice house and none of the interior rooms had doors; they only had sheets hanging from the door frames. When Jep walked in, he said, "I love this! No doors!" Then he went flying through the sheets pretending to be a superhero.

Jep did not see the person's lack. He saw something fun. He saw value in what some people would have viewed as a deficiency. He is still that way, and I try to be too. My grandparents have never had a lot, materially speaking, but they have worked hard all their lives, and they are wonderful people whom I dearly love and am so close to. Jep and I make a concentrated effort not to pay attention to economic differences, even when they are very obvious. We want to value and appreciate each person we come in contact with, and we want to teach our children to do the same.

I still remember when Jep and I spent our weekends at outdoor shows, selling duck calls to make extra money. Even in those days, people lined up to get Phil's autograph. Now people ask *us* for our autographs, and sometimes we can hardly believe it.

Being in the limelight has brought us both blessings and challenges, but if we lose everything tomorrow, we will still be happy. We can be confident of that because we were happy before we had it. We believe that the more we have, the more we can share, and that's what we are determined to do.

Of course, the television show has made some things easier. We still live in the same house we have lived in for years, but we did finally get a new vehicle. I am still a serious bargain shopper, and I still go through the clearance racks, but we can now afford a few more groceries, and we can have people over to our house more often. We can definitely serve people more effectively

> The more we have, the more we can share, and that's what we are determined to do. —*Jessica*

and meet more of the needs around us. We do not have as much time as we used to, but we make the most of what we do have. I am diligent about being at home with the kids in the afternoons, and we still make a priority of family time together. In the end, that is what's important to us and that's what we most want to preserve.

29

GREAT REWARDS

Korie

I married Willie thinking he was clean-cut and preppy. When we got married, he had short hair and no beard. And he did not dip. He was the "city boy" among the Robertson men. On the other hand, Jase was outdoorsy. He spent his time in the woods or on the river—hunting, fishing, catching frogs, or doing other things connected to outdoor life—like Phil. The Willie I married was headed in a totally different direction from Phil and Jase. He wanted to do his own thing, chart his own course. If I could only tell you about all the businesses Willie has dreamed of starting, all the jobs he was going to have, from professional golfer to karaoke deejay! Willie has always thought big. He has also always enjoyed hunting, but early in our marriage he thought he would do something different from his dad. I had no idea that all these years later, he would become so much like Phil he would practically turn into his dad and that our family would appear each week on a television show centered around duck calls and hunting.

Phil and Willie are a lot alike. Even Miss Kay says that. They are both strong-minded, visionary, and entrepreneurial. Phil started Duck Commander and grew it to a certain point with a lot of hard work and determination. When Willie got involved in the business, he saw all kinds of ways to expand it. He and I eventually took a leap of faith and bought a portion of the business from Phil, never dreaming it would take our family to prime time.

> I married Willie thinking he was clean-cut and preppy. —*Korie*

The Robertson men have been involved in media for years, much longer than some people realize. They started with hunting videos that appealed primarily to serious hunters. Because of those, Phil especially became well known among certain audiences, but nothing like he is now. Ten years ago, he and Willie could have walked through Times Square and no one would have noticed them—well, except for Phil's beard and rough look. That would not be the case today!

Being on the show has given us so many opportunities we never thought we would have. As a family, we enjoy doing live appearances together, and we have been involved in some really fun things. Sometimes, when we all pack up to travel to a live appearance, we feel like we are going on a field trip. Those times often provide our children with chances to do things Willie and I never imagined they would be able to do. For example, we had a great time when we all participated in the 2013 Country Music Association Awards. John

Luke and Sadie even got to introduce Dierks Bentley, which was fun for all of us to see.

GREAT PEOPLE, GOOD NEWS

One of the best blessings of the visibility *Duck Dynasty* has provided us is the chance to interact with so many great people. Our fans are terrific and we enjoy getting a minute to chat with them whenever we can. We also have opportunities to meet talented, dedicated people who are doing some amazing work, mostly projects or initiatives to serve others by relieving suffering, offering tangible hope, transforming communities, or finding other ways to make an impact in this world. We are often invited to grand openings or fund-raisers for these kinds of activities, and I love seeing how creative, passionate, and determined some people are to do good and to bless others.

Unfortunately, the news these days is full of negativity, sad stories, and flat-out bad reporting. Because our show has given us a platform to travel and meet people, we have learned that there is also quite a bit of good news in the world. Many people we meet are doing interesting and wonderful things that do not receive any news coverage. Once we started traveling, we realized quickly that the positive things happening in the world are highly underreported!

We cannot possibly say yes to every invitation we receive; there simply are not enough hours in the day. But we try to do as much as we can to help various charities. One of my favorite stories involves an organization that was trying to build a park with a playground for children with special needs. They needed to raise one hundred thousand dollars to build the park. We attended their fund-raiser, and when it was over, they were shocked and excited to have hit their mark in one night! We were so glad our presence provoked so much generosity and so happy to know the children were going to have a nice place to play. We really enjoy being involved in things like this.

DUCK DYNASTY IS MAKING A DIFFERENCE

Doing what we do does take a lot out of us at times, but it's worth it. Our busy schedules and frequent travel can be tiring, but they provide us with so much fulfillment. What is most fulfilling for me is hearing stories from fans about the positive impact *Duck Dynasty* and our family have had on their lives and their families. We have had people tell us with tears in their eyes that the show has brought their family closer together, and we love that—because close-knit family is what we're all about. One woman told us she and her husband had not been able to find a single television show to watch together in more than fifteen years—until *Duck Dynasty*. People also tell us their pastors preach about the show on Sundays, using lessons from the show to help people grow in their faith.

Maybe the most meaningful thing of all to us is that families have started praying together as a result of the dinner scenes at the conclusion of most *Duck Dynasty* episodes. We have even heard of one group of fifth graders who call themselves the "Duck Dynasty Club." They sit together during lunch at school every day and pray before their meal. We feel so blessed to be part of these good things that are happening because of one TV show. We had no idea it would make such an impact.

When we first started doing *Duck Dynasty*, several people asked us if our faith would play a part in it. We thought that was kind of an odd question, because we do not know how to separate our faith from everything else we do. Faith is how we live; it's who we are. No one can take it out of us. If anyone is going to do a show about us, they will also get our faith.

So much about today's entertainment industry is based on shock value. Every season, it seems like networks make an effort to push the envelope a little more in terms of sex, violence, and language. When we went on television, we presented an alternative. People can find disrespectful spouses, disobedient children, and bad language on other shows; they will not get it from us because that's not the way we live. Some people have been surprised at our success; others are simply grateful to have a family-centered show that keeps the language clean, affirms traditional values, and honors God in every episode.

> **We do not know how to separate our faith from everything else we do.**
>
> —*Korie*

WE CAN'T WORRY ABOUT WHAT PEOPLE THINK

One of the most important lessons I have learned about living a very public life is that we cannot pay too much attention to what people think or say about us. I actually learned this lesson a long time ago, because everyone deals with this throughout his or her life to some extent. But the issue is magnified when you have a hit television show. Still, it's a lesson for everyone. Whether it happens in school, at church, or in the workplace, people are going to be critical of the things you do, what you wear, the choices you make, or something else. You cannot control that; all you can control is what you do and how you live. And if you are living to please God, that's all that matters.

Our family cannot control the press we get, but when it's inaccurate or when it simply does not tell the whole story about us, we do not have to let it upset us. I remember a specific incident that took this thought to a whole new level for John Luke and made it personal for all of us.

John Luke was out with his friends, a group of guys, in Willie's truck. I should have known when they left our house to send a girl with them; there was way too much testosterone in that vehicle! While they were out, they saw an old, beat-up boat on the riverbank (it even had bullet holes in it). It had been there for years, but for some reason it caught their attention that day and John Luke decided to bring it home. It was waterlogged and full of junk, so the boys spent hours pulling it out of the river. They then loaded it on a trailer, not realizing there is a limit to how much weight a trailer can haul.

Feeling pretty good about themselves, the boys climbed into the truck, rolled down the windows, and headed home. They were living the life, just having fun. As John Luke rounded a corner, the weight of the boat was too much for the truck and the trailer. The truck flipped four times. To look at the wreckage, a person would think no one survived. But thank God, no one was seriously hurt. John Luke crawled out of that truck without a scratch on him, and the boys in the backseat—who were not even wearing their seat belts—had only a couple of bumps and bruises. It was a miracle, and we still thank God for protecting those guys.

When Willie and I heard about the accident, like any parents, we rushed to the scene to make sure they were all okay. When people passing by noticed us, they stopped, and soon a crowd had gathered. The police eventually had to ask us to leave. We hated to do that, but we understood we were attracting too much attention. The police had a hard time doing their job with so many people around.

I didn't even notice at the time because I was too focused on the boys being okay, but the policemen pointed out that the boat had been full of empty beer cans that were now strewn across the road. We all knew the boys had not been drinking, but the policeman was concerned for us that people might jump to the wrong conclusion and that the news might pick that up and report it.

I used those circumstances to reinforce a lesson Willie and I have been teaching our children for years. We tell them not to ever worry about what people think, especially when those people do not even know them. We help them understand that people often make judgments based on wrong or incomplete information, so we cannot worry about that either. All we need to care about is what God thinks and what the people who know us and love us think. We do our best to live lives that are pleasing to God, and we do not pay much attention to the rest.

When I was John Luke's or Sadie's age, no one had ever heard of social media. But now, while many of the responses we get through social media or the press are positive, there are times when I'm appalled by what people post about our family. A lot of it is not true, and some of it is downright hateful, so we just delete it and do not give it a second thought. It's a lot easier for me to say this at my age than it is for my children to believe it as teenagers, so I make sure to reinforce this continuously. Social media and the press can work the other way too; you can read all the great things people say about you and get a little too big for your britches fast, if you are not careful. I can say for sure that ever since *Duck Dynasty* started, all of us Robertsons have gotten really good at ignoring what certain people think or say! We focus on honoring God and living godly lives with our family and friends. At the end of the day, when the spotlight turns away from us and on to the next thing, those are the people who will be there for us. We will always appreciate our fans, but our family will be the ones we turn to when we need wisdom, comfort, or just plain old help.

ALL GOOD THINGS MUST COME TO AN END

I try to look at this *Duck Dynasty* time in our lives as one season of many seasons to come. I am enjoying this one, but I look forward to different seasons in the future, which we can enjoy for different reasons. I know we will not live in the limelight forever. Television shows all have a life span. Even television's most popular, longest-running shows eventually come to an end. We know ours will too. Maybe, when that time comes, the guys will shave their beards and cut their hair, and we'll ride off into the sunset.

Part Seven

INQUIRING MINDS
WANT TO KNOW

Your word is a lamp to my feet and a light to my path.

PSALM 119:105, NKJV

INTRODUCTION

Korie

Everywhere we go, people ask us questions. Sometimes the questions—and their answers—are really funny; sometimes they are very serious. They want to know everything from whether we like our husbands' beards to how we juggle busy schedules to whether they can have Miss Kay's biscuit recipe (which is included in this section). They ask us how we keep our children grounded and whether or not Uncle Si really is everything he seems to be. They also ask about our faith and about what it's like to have such a large family.

If you have a question we don't answer, maybe we'll see you in our travels one of these days and you can ask us then! —*Korie*

Sometimes, girls ask me if they can marry John Luke or guys ask me if they can have Sadie's phone number. I'll go ahead and answer those now: no and no.

Before we finish this book, we want to address some of the most common questions we receive. Some of those questions are directed to a specific person; others are ones we all want to comment on. I hope you will get to know us even better through these last pages, and if you have a question we don't answer, maybe we'll see you in our travels one of these days and you can ask us then!

ANSWERS TO THE TWENTY
QUESTIONS PEOPLE ASK US MOST

1. Do you like the beards?

Miss Kay: If Phil ever shaved his beard, I'd think I was committing adultery.

Korie: When I married Willie, he was clean-shaven and had short hair. Boy, how things change! Over the years, I've really come to like the look he has now, including the beard.

Missy: I love Jase. I don't like the beard. I miss the days of scratch-free kisses. Besides, he's just too cute under there!

Jessica: Yes! Although Jep is really cute under all that hair, and although he does have the Robertson dimples, I still prefer the beard. I think sometime over the course of our marriage I transitioned to loving the beard. I do make him trim the mustache every once in a while for better kisses! I also feel safer with the beard; I know no one is going to mess with us because the beard kind of scares people. For some reason, I think they think he's a madman!

Lisa: Alan is often referred to as "the Robertson without a beard," and I like it that way!

2. Tell us the truth about Uncle Si.

Lisa: Si is one of the most gracious people in our family. He is willing to do almost everything I ask him to do. He has a soft spot for kids. He is a kind, generous, and loving man. He loves his wife, his children, and his eight grandsons. Si is a little eccentric, but he is a lot of fun to be in a family with.

Korie: When Willie and I travel and get to interact with our fans, someone almost always asks us, "Where's Si?" People just love him! I usually give the same answer every time: "Taking a nap." I figure if I say that at any given time, there's a very good chance it's true!

Jessica: Si is one of the sweetest men I have ever known. He is such a great uncle to the kids in our family, and in fact, all kids seem to love him. I have *never* heard him say a negative word about anyone—and I mean *anyone*. He has the biggest heart!

Missy: The specific question people most often ask me is "Is Si really as crazy as he seems?" Yes.

3. Miss Kay, you seem like a very wise woman. What's your secret?

Miss Kay: All I know to do is just live by what the Bible says is right and wrong. It's that simple. To me, the only way to raise a family is to do what the Bible says to do. People often want me to talk about family values or say that *Duck Dynasty* is based on family values. But, plain and simple, family values come from the Bible. My parents and grandparents taught my sister and me how to

> Plain and simple, family values come from the Bible.
> —*Miss Kay*

behave, about respecting other people, about forgiveness, and about discipline when we were very young. All those things come from the Bible, and I'm so thankful I was raised to live by what the Bible says. I did the same for my boys.

I love God's Word and I have a lot of favorite Bible verses. The one I call my "clutch verse"—because of the way I hung on to it through the bad years—is Philippians 4:13: "I can do all things through Christ who strengthens me" (NKJV). Another one of my favorites is Proverbs 22:6: "Train up a child in the way he should go, and when he is old he will not depart from it" (NKJV). I did my best to teach my boys what God says when they were very young. Even though a couple of them had rebellious seasons, they all came back to their roots of faith. Now that they are older, they have not departed from the lessons they learned as children.

4. Korie, is Miss Kay's cooking really that good, and is yours really that bad?

Korie: The answer is yes and yes. I have never eaten anything from Miss Kay's table that I didn't like. She really enjoys cooking, and she loves watching people enjoy what she cooks. She is the kind of mom who gets her feelings hurt if you come to her house not hungry. If you show up there at dinnertime, you'd better at least take a bite and let her know how good it is!

I, on the other hand, always seem to have too many things going on to be a good cook. I really tried in our early years of marriage, but I would get distracted and burn the bread or put apple cinnamon muffin mix in the corn casserole instead of corn bread mix (true story) and ruin the entire dish. Corn and cinnamon do *not* go together. I've learned to accept that there are other things I'm good at and leave the cooking to Willie in our house.

5. Jessica, you have four young children. How do you juggle it all?

Jessica: Well, lots of prayer. God is my strength! And with being blessed with such a large family, we lean on each other for support. As a family, we help each other out. When I am gone, I can call on any one of my sisters-in-law or on Miss Kay to help, and they know they can call on me any time they need me. I also have great parents who help out a lot. And we have one babysitter who has been with us since Lily (our oldest child) was little. She is more like a family member than a babysitter; the kids view her as a big sister.

6. Missy, who's the better shot: you or Jase?

Missy: The quick and obvious answer is Jase. He is well known for his accuracy (even though Si claims he shoots all the ducks). However, I love to share this story: On the last day of duck season 2012, Jase took Mia and me on a late-afternoon duck hunt. Mia was shooting BBs at the decoys and Jase and I were waiting for the last run of ducks to come through for the year when two ducks came flying over from right to left. We both fired when they got in front of us. He aimed for the front one, and I aimed for the back one, and the back one fell. Jase missed. It was a glorious hunt.

7. Lisa, does the entire Robertson family *really* vacation together?

Lisa: Well, almost everyone. We call it EBP, "Everybody but Phil." He stays home because he simply does not understand what we love about the beach. The things he doesn't like, we love—such as sand and sun. There are thirty of us, and we try to rent a large house or a duplex when we vacation. We lead very busy lives, and even though we film together, we also love to go and just let our hair down and have fun together. The guys golf almost every day, while the ladies sun and shop.

8. Are the Robertson kids really as respectful and obedient as they seem?

All: Yes. We have raised them to respect and obey their elders. They are all typical kids, but respect is one of the core values of our family and they truly are respectful kids.

9. Korie, what's your favorite episode of *Duck Dynasty*?

Korie: This is a hard one because there are a lot of episodes I love, but I think my favorite is "Driving Miss Sadie." It's fun to see what happens when I'm not around, like hearing the driving advice Si gave Sadie. Plus, it's like having really great home videos of milestones in our children's lives.

10. Lisa, why do the boys call their parents "Kay" and "Phil" instead of "Mom" and "Dad"?

Lisa: I am not sure anyone remembers exactly how the boys started calling their parents by their first names, but I have a couple of ideas.

For one thing, during the boys' formative years, when Granny and Pa lived next door to Phil and Miss Kay, the entire family worked together, ate together, and enjoyed very close relationships. Phil called Granny "Mom" and Pa "Dad," so maybe having two people called "Mom" and two called "Dad" was too confusing. Granny and Pa called Phil and Kay by their first names, so maybe the boys picked it up from them.

The other reason it may have started is that for a lot of years, Phil and Miss Kay ran their own business. The boys helped them in all kinds of ways. When dealing with customers and vendors, using first names for every employee is more professional than calling the boss "Dad." They would not have said to someone who called, "Yes, you may speak to my mom," but "Yes, you may speak to Kay."

Sometimes people think the boys are being disrespectful by calling Phil and Kay by their first names. The important thing is that Phil and Miss Kay do not think it's disrespectful at all. They know how much the boys respect them, and they do not need to be called by any particular terms to prove it. Miss Kay likes to say, "I'm fine with them calling me 'Kay' as long as they call me!"

11. Jessica, what's it like being married to a serious hunter?

Jessica: It's definitely not like having a husband with a nine-to-five job! A lot of marriages and families have to adjust to whatever a spouse does for a living. People who are married to doctors, soldiers, firefighters, or others all have to find a way to make life work in the midst of unusual schedules. One difference between us and some of our friends is that hunting is part of the job for Robertson men. Sure, they enjoy it, but it's also how they make a living. There were times when duck hunting and the things that go with it were the *only* way they made a living. So, hunting is not a hobby in our family; it is part of our livelihood.

All of us wives know we will not see as much of our husbands during duck season as we do at other times of the year. For example, during duck season, Jep gets up and leaves the house at about four o'clock in the morning and does not return until about six o'clock at night. When he gets home, he is exhausted. His day may have included not only hunting but also filming, editing, and producing hunting videos, because those are also part of his job responsibilities.

During duck season, I have had to learn to let him rest when he gets home and to find creative things to do with our children while he is away. We all miss him when he's gone so much of the time, so he and I have had to find ways to make the most of the time we do have together during hunting season, which isn't much. Thankfully, my sisters-in-law and Miss Kay understand this well. We're all in the same boat!

12. Missy, did you ever think your life would turn out like this?
Missy: Never in my wildest dreams. I knew I wanted to be used by God in big ways. I always prayed He would trust me enough to use me to make a difference in His Kingdom, but I never dreamed it would be through a cable television show, the number one cable television show in A&E network history, as of this writing! Ephe-

sians 3:20–21 best describes how I feel: "Now to him who is able to do immeasurably more than all we ask or imagine, according to his power that is at work within us, to him be glory in the church and in Christ Jesus throughout all generations, for ever and ever! Amen." It is not because of any power or wisdom we possess that this happened. It is all because of His power, His power working through us. What a dream come true!

13. Miss Kay, may I have your biscuit recipe?

Miss Kay: Sure! Here it is, and you can find more great recipes of mine in my cookbook, *Miss Kay's Duck Commander Kitchen.*

Homemade Biscuits

2 cups Pioneer Original Biscuit and Baking Mix,
   plus a little extra
1 cup sour cream
½ cup Sprite or 7 Up
1 stick of butter

Mix all ingredients except butter with a pie blender (pastry blender).

Pour a little biscuit mix on wax paper.

Put a cup of dough in the middle of the biscuit mix.

Form a ball and pat it down so you can cut the biscuits with a glass.

Cut just enough to fill a skillet or cake pan with biscuits (I use a skillet).

Melt a stick of butter in a skillet or cake pan.

Roll biscuits in butter and place them in the pan.

Bake at 375 degrees until brown.

14. Lisa, what are some of the things for which you have heard the boys really got in trouble when they were younger?

Lisa: I have always heard the boys got in big trouble for three things: disrespecting their mother, tearing up good equipment (whether that was a fishing pole, a rifle, or something in the house), and coming to blows with each other. They did not get punished for disagreeing with each other, and disagreements were common I'm sure. But if a conflict escalated to the point that fists started swinging, then they got punished. Standard punishment in the Robertson household was three licks.

When people comment on the fact that they got in trouble for disrespecting their mother but not for disrespecting their father, Alan likes to say with a chuckle, "Who would want to disrespect Phil, as good a shot as he is?"

> The boys got in big trouble for three things: disrespecting their mother, tearing up good equipment, and coming to blows with each other. —*Lisa*

15. What is Christmas like for the Robertson family?

Miss Kay: It's a Cajun seafood feast!

Korie: One of the most fun things about Christmas with the Robertsons is that Miss Kay makes us laugh with her gifts. She loves to buy gag gifts, and she puts cards on them saying these gifts are from the dogs or from someone famous. For example, she would buy a gigantic bra and give it to one of us with a card saying, "Merry

Christmas from Dolly Parton." She once had a dog named Doogie Howser, and one year she gave Missy a plastic pile of dog poop from Doogie. The funniest thing about her gag gifts, though, is when people open a present and get a quizzical look on their face because they can't figure out the joke (not all of the gag gifts are as obvious as Dolly Parton's), and Miss Kay bursts out laughing because she can't remember why she thought it was funny. We think *that* is even funnier than her gifts!

16. Missy, how do you keep your kids grounded?

Missy: Jase and I have what I like to call "Come to Jesus Meetings" whenever we feel the need. Jase is the kind of person who does not like to let things go without being settled. I was raised quite differently. Neither my parents nor I are confrontational people, so we usually just waited for things to get better on their own or work themselves out. Sometimes they did; sometimes they didn't. Not so with a Robertson.

Jase will analyze each behavior, good or bad, until the issue is completely resolved. This is a great quality when it comes to parenting, and even though it was against my nature, I gladly jumped on board, especially when I saw the end results. When we see bad behavior or potential bad behavior with our kids, we sit down and figure out the problem. Many nights have been spent in our living room with Bibles open and notebooks in hand while we hash out what's going on. Bad behavior doesn't just happen on its own. Something unresolved is going on in their lives that fuels that bad behavior.

With our teenage boys, most of the issues have revolved around bad choices in their friendships. Teenage boys love to be admired and given positive attention. Teenage girls have figured this out, godly girls and ungodly girls. It's our job as parents to make sure our boys are associating with people who want what's best for them, not what's best for themselves. And when your kids are stars on a national television show, there is definitely a big difference. I have to be very skeptical about new friendships in order to protect them.

17. Jessica, why weren't you and Jep on the show more during its early seasons?

Jessica: Well, it really wasn't up to us. I appreciate and love all the time we are all together as a family filming *Duck Dynasty*, and I think everything happens for a reason, in God's perfect timing. As our kids get a little older, juggling filming and the demands of raising four children gets a little easier! We have to keep our priorities straight.

18. Korie, is Sadie really that bad of a driver?

Korie: She went to driver's ed, and now she's actually really good. I think she's better than John Luke!

19. Does everyone in the family really get along as well as you appear to get along on *Duck Dynasty*?

All: We get so many questions about the way we live our lives. People wonder if we really are nice to each other and if we really can get through a day or a week without someone shouting or erupting in anger. We do not have very sophisticated answers. All we can say is that we do our best to live with integrity, character, and a strong value system—the way God wants us to live. We take our instructions from the Good Book, the Word of God. We do not just read it; we seek to apply its principles to every area of our everyday lives—doing business, raising children, building marriages, dealing with interpersonal relationships, managing our time and money, and more. So far, it's worked pretty well for us!

20. How long will *Duck Dynasty* last?

All: We don't know, but we are enjoying it while it does, and we hope it will go on for as long as it is part of God's plan for our lives. We love and appreciate all of our fans and hope every episode will bring love, laughter, and a renewed sense of faith and family to everyone who watches.

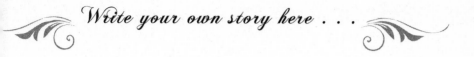

Write your own story here . . .

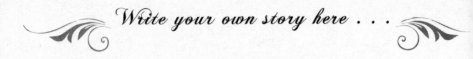

Write your own story here . . .

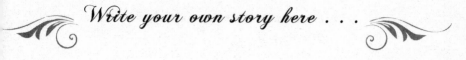

Write your own story here . . .

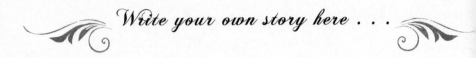

Write your own story here . . .

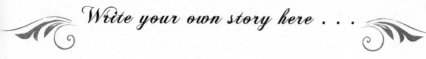 *Write your own story here . . .*

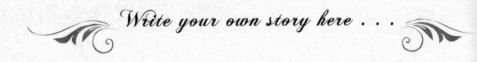

Write your own story here . . .

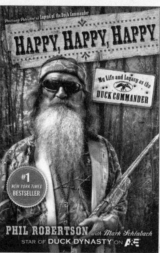